HEALTHY Vegan Kids

Everything you need to know about vegan diets for children

By Juliet Gellatley, founder & director of Viva! and nutritional therapist and Veronika Charvátová, Viva! Health researcher

© Viva! 2022
Registered charity 1037486

Produced by:
Viva!, 8 York Court, Wilder St, Bristol BS2 8QH
Tel: 0117 944 1000
E: info@viva.org.uk

More info on Healthy Vegan Kids at **viva.org.uk/children**

viva.org.uk
viva.org.uk/health
veganrecipeclub.org.uk
 vivavegancharity
 vivacampaigns
vivacharity

Juliet Gellatley BSc, Dip CNM, Dip DM, FNTP, NTCC
Juliet has a degree in zoology and is a qualified nutritional therapist. She founded and directs Viva! and is an authority on vegan health and nutrition.

She is the mum of twin sons (Jazz and Finn) and understands the challenges involved in helping kids be healthy eaters! She has given hundreds of public talks on all the vegan issues and is author of several books and reports.

Veronika Charvátová MSc
Veronika is a biologist and Viva! Health researcher. She has been uncovering the links between nutrition and health for over a decade and is an expert on plant-based diets. She's also a step-mum to two fussy eaters and knows the struggle of making sure that children are well-fed.

Contents

World Turned Upside Down!..6
What Does Vegetarian and Vegan Mean? 8
What Foods Should Children Eat? 9
What Foods Do Children Eat? 10
Left Unprotected 12
What Children Should Eat Each Day to Be Fit and Healthy 14
Eat Vegan – Live Longer 16
Lethal Double Whammy 17
Vegan Kids are Healthier 18
Healthy Foods for Children 20
5 A DAY For Kids: How Much Do They Need?..............22
Winning Tips for 5 A DAY for Kids 25
Recipe Ideas 27
Every Nutrient a Child Needs and How to Get It 29
Vegan Eatwell Plate for Children 44
How Animal Products Affect Children 45
How Animal Products Affect Adults 55
Children's Eating Habits 71
Conclusions 72
References 73

World Turned upside down!

Just imagine if you read of a diet that produced these headlines:

"Heart disease rates tumble! 40,000 heart patients taken off critical list – misery lifted for relatives and friends. Top heart surgeon says most heart ops avoidable."

"Cancer deaths slump!"

"Millions not obese anymore."

"Diabetes figures fall for the first time."

"Food poisoning cases tumble – records no longer worth maintaining."

What diet could it possibly be? That's easy! The same diet that children should be eating now so they enjoy good health throughout their lives – a well-balanced vegan diet.

If statistics were reversed and most of the population became vegan, these headlines could become a reality. Unbelievable isn't it? The scientific evidence to justify them is there in abundance and this guide shows just how strong it is.

> *"People stumble over the truth from time to time, but most pick themselves up and hurry off as if nothing happened."*
> Sir Winston Churchill

One thing is certain, research showing that a meat-based diet reduces cancer risk or cuts heart disease by up to a half doesn't exist. It does for healthy vegan diets. One by one, the world's leading health advisory bodies have confirmed that avoiding animal products and eating plenty of unrefined plant foods is the way to greatly reduce the risk of many diseases, and that includes the growing threat from obesity.

> *"Although human beings eat meat, we are not natural carnivores. No matter how much fat carnivores eat, they do not develop atherosclerosis [clogged up arteries]. When we kill animals to eat them, they end up killing us because their flesh, which contains cholesterol and saturated fat, was never intended for human beings, who are natural herbivores."*
> Dr WC Roberts, Editor-in-chief of the American Journal of Cardiology

So, what's all this got to do with your little'uns – those fussy eaters, messy eaters, must-have-chips-with-everything eaters?

Every leading health advisory body is saying the same thing – what you feed your children today will determine their health in the future. And it isn't going to change because the science is now just too overwhelming.

But fear not! By opening this guide, you've already taken the first step in the right direction. It will take you through the science, much of which may be new to you. Why? Because of the power of the vested interests who profit from meat, fish and dairy. If you think we're exaggerating, remember the tobacco industry. The damage that smoking does to human health has been known since the 1950s but it took decades before serious action was taken against it.

What does vegetarian and vegan mean?

A vegetarian doesn't eat red meat, white meat (poultry such as chicken, duck and turkey), fish or other water life (prawns, lobsters, crabs, shellfish) or slaughterhouse by-products (gelatine, animal fat, lard or animal rennet). Most vegetarians are 'lacto-ovo', which means they don't eat meat or fish but do eat dairy products and eggs. Viva!'s definition of vegan is: Vegans don't eat, wear or use anything from animals — whether from land animals (meat, dairy, eggs, honey, shellac, leather, fur etc) or from water animals (fish, prawns, crab, lobster etc). Vegans also exclude, as far as is practicable, all forms of animal exploitation and cruelty.

Although excluding things sounds as though we're restricting our choices, in fact it's the opposite. Most meaty diets are based on just three main food types – meat, dairy and wheat. By giving them different names, we kid ourselves we're eating a huge variety but we're not. Pork, beef, chicken and lamb are in the same food group; cheese, yoghurt, ice-cream and butter are in the same; and bread, rolls, buns, baps, crispbread, pasta, pies, pasties, cakes and 'baked goods' are in the same. Whichever way you list them, it's still just three food types.

This isn't the case with plant foods – they are not one or two food groups but several more health-giving ones. Diets based on plant foods include hundreds of vegetables, fruits, nuts, seeds, grains and pulses. Judge plant-based diets on what is included not what's excluded and you'll see them through different eyes.

What foods should children eat?

Animal products promote disease. They are rich in blood-vessel-clogging saturated fats, contain too much animal protein, have no fibre, no starchy carbohydrates, little or no vitamins C, E or beta-carotene (the precursor to vitamin A).

A lack of these vitamins and fibre, and excess of saturated fat, animal protein and cholesterol are risk factors for many types of cancer, heart disease, stroke, high blood pressure, diabetes, obesity, gallstones and several other diseases. A meat or cheese-based lunchbox is not the healthiest by any stretch of the imagination.

A varied, plant-based lunch-box full of fresh fruit and vegetables, beans, wholegrains, nuts and seeds is bursting with all the ingredients known to be health promoting and health protecting.

There's loads of protein in beans, lentils, chickpeas, soya, nuts and seeds. Vegan diets also contain essential ('good') fats, fibre, starchy carbohydrates (the good carbs!), antioxidant vitamins and minerals – all that's needed to stay fit and healthy. (See pages 14-15.)

What foods do children eat?

There is an ongoing survey by the UK government's Public Health England, called The National Diet and Nutrition Survey Rolling Programme. In 2020, they published the results of the eating habits of young people aged 1.5 to 18 years in Great Britain, collected between 2016 and 2019 (PHE, 2020).

It probably comes as no surprise to most parents but makes for grim reading nevertheless. For example, it revealed that children eat more than twice as much sugar as they should. That means sweets of all kind, sweetened drinks, biscuits and chocolate.

These are some of the main findings of the survey:

- All children eat too much saturated fat (bad for the heart)
- Most children eat too little fibre (important to keep the digestive system healthy)
- Only 12 per cent meet the recommended 5 A DAY fruit and vegetable intake

- Around a half of all children don't get enough iron and folate
- About a fifth of children over 11 years of age lack vitamin D
- And around 15 per cent lack sufficient calcium

This goes to show that any diet needs to be well-planned to provide all that children need – meat-eating children don't automatically get enough vital nutrients and eat too much fat and sugar.

As for physical activity – important for healthy bone development and prevention of diseases – many boys and girls have less than the recommended one hour per day.

It's clear that a large proportion of children are lacking many of the vital nutrients needed to help combat disease. They are eating a diet high in fat, salt and sugar largely due to convenience foods based on processed meat, white flour and dairy products.

Fresh fruit and vegetables, along with healthy energy-rich starchy foods such as wholegrain cereals, wholegrain breads, wholewheat pasta and brown rice, all take a back seat when it comes to young people's dinner plates, if they appear at all. Sadly, children are likely to suffer the consequences in terms of poor health and a reduced quality of life.

World Cancer Research Fund (2018) published a set of recommendations for maintaining good health and preventing cancer. These are:

- Be a healthy weight
- Be physically active
- Eat a diet rich in wholegrains, vegetables, fruit and beans
- Limit consumption of 'fast foods' and other processed foods high in fat, starches or sugars
- Limit consumption of red and processed meat
- Limit consumption of sugar-sweetened drinks
- Limit alcohol consumption
- Do not use supplements for cancer prevention (aim to meet nutritional needs though diet)

They state that these recommendations would also lower the risk of many other non-infectious diseases, such as heart disease, diabetes and obesity. All we need to do is tweak our diets and it's best to start early in life.

Research shows that vegan children typically have higher quality diets compared with their peers, with a healthier intake of fat – less saturated and more unsaturated fats, more fruit and vegetables, less junk food, salt and fizzy drinks and their diets contain much less harmful substances usually found in animal foods (Amit, 2010; Melina *et al.*, 2016).

Left unprotected

Imagine finding out that your child was smoking regularly. You'd be understandably horrified – and why? Because it's now known that smoking is one of the leading causes of cancer deaths in adults – responsible for over seven million premature deaths a year (GBD 2017 Risk Factor Collaborators, 2018). Less known is that even more premature deaths – about 11 million a year globally – are caused by a bad diet (GBD 2017 Diet Collaborators, 2019).

The good news is that by changing your and your children's diet to wholefood vegan, you can help protect yourselves from many chronic diseases. Have a look at the table on page nine for what a young teenager should eat each day for energy, zest and good health!

"It is the position of the Academy of Nutrition and Dietetics that appropriately planned vegetarian, including vegan, diets are healthful, nutritionally adequate, and may provide health benefits for the prevention and treatment of certain diseases. These diets are appropriate for all stages of the life cycle, including pregnancy, lactation, infancy, childhood, adolescence, older adulthood, and for athletes."

"Vegetarian children and teens are at lower risk than their non-vegetarian peers for overweight and obesity. Children and adolescents with BMI values in the normal range are more likely to also be within the normal range as adults, resulting in significant disease risk reduction. Other benefits of a vegetarian diet in childhood and adolescence include greater consumption of fruits and vegetables, fewer sweets and salty snacks, and lower intakes of total and saturated fat. Consuming balanced vegetarian diets early in life can establish healthful lifelong habits."
Academy of Nutrition and Dietetics (Melina *et al.*, 2016)

What children should eat each day to be fit and healthy

This chart is for 12-year-olds or older children; younger ones require the same foods but in smaller serving sizes.

NO. OF SERVINGS	At least 5
FOODS	Fruit and vegetables
TO PROVIDE	Healthy energy, vitamin A, vitamin C, vitamin K, folate, calcium, iron, fibre and many antioxidants!

HEALTHY SERVING SIZE

Fresh fruit	1 medium piece – the size of a tennis ball
Dried fruit	1-1½ tablespoons or the size of a golf ball
Green or root veg	3 tablespoons
Salad veg	80 grams or a large cereal bowl

NO. OF SERVINGS	3-5
FOODS	Wholegrains and cereals
TO PROVIDE	Energy, fibre, B vitamins, calcium, iron, protein

HEALTHY SERVING SIZE

Cooked brown rice, couscous or other grains	2-3 heaped tablespoons or ½ cup
Breakfast cereal	1 regular-sized cereal bowl
Wholewheat pasta	1 cup (cooked) as side dish or 2 cups as main dish
Wholemeal bread	2 slices

3

NO. OF SERVINGS 3-4
FOODS Pulses, nuts or seeds
TO PROVIDE Protein, energy, healthy fats, fibre, calcium, iron, other minerals and antioxidants

HEALTHY SERVING SIZE

Peas, beans, chickpeas and lentils	½ cup (cooked)
Tofu, mock meats, burgers, sausages	100 grams or one serving (burger or sausage)
Nuts or seeds	2 tablespoons or a small handful

4

NO. OF SERVINGS Small amounts
FOODS Healthy oils
TO PROVIDE Energy, vitamin E (vegetable oils), vitamins A & D (fortified margarine), essential omega-3 and omega-6 fats (flaxseed, walnut, hemp)

HEALTHY SERVING SIZE

Flaxseed, hempseed, walnut oil	1 tbsp used cold
Rapeseed oil	1 tbsp for cooking
Virgin olive oil	1 tbsp used cold
Plant-based margarine	Small amounts

5

NO. OF SERVINGS Daily dose
FOODS Vitamin B12, Vitamin D
HEALTHY SERVING SIZE These are vital to give as supplements – 50 micrograms of vitamin B12 and 10 micrograms of vitamin D

FOODS Omega-3 fats
HEALTHY SERVING SIZE 1 tsp flaxseed oil / 1tbsp ground flaxseed or chia seeds / 2 tbsp of hempseed / 10 walnut halves. Children aged 1-3 should get a daily omega-3 supplement made from algae

Aim for one to two litres of water each day. Add a slice of lemon, other fruit or fresh mint. Squash can contribute but unsweetened drinks (eg fruit or herbal tea) are better.

Eat vegan – live longer

Many of the ailments we associate with old age are not a result of getting older but are caused by eating the wrong foods throughout our life. High blood pressure is a good example – often seen as inevitable in old people. Yet in countries where a plant-based diet is the norm, this simply isn't the case.

A massive piece of research looked at the diets of over 73,000 people over a period of several years and found that vegans have a 15 per cent lower risk of premature death than meat-eaters (Orlich *et al.*, 2013). They live longer!

Another large study found that people whose diets contained the most fruit, vegetables, nuts, cereals, pulses, olive oil and potatoes and the least animal fats, eggs, fish, dairy products, meat and meat products were 41 per cent less likely to die early, compared with the rest of the population (Martínez-González *et al.*, 2014).

One study actually calculated that to prevent several million premature deaths every year globally, everyone should include 800 grams of fruits and vegetables, 225 grams of wholegrains and 15-20 grams of nuts in their daily diet (Aune, 2019).

If we ate only meat and cow's milk, we would die – and pretty quickly. If we ate only plant foods, we would be likely to live for a very long time. People on the Japanese island of Okinawa are among the longest-lived and healthiest people in the world. One of the most important factors is their diet – based on wholegrains, vegetables, fruits and soya products. One of their favourite foods has been dubbed 'immortal pâté'. It is vegan and based on tofu (soya bean curd), miso (fermented soya paste), mushrooms and garlic. It tastes as good as the good it does you!

Lethal double whammy

Today's younger generation is facing a potentially lethal, diet-related double whammy thanks to a diet centred around animal products.

Disease statistics are alarming and although previous generations may have had their own problems, rampant heart disease, obesity and cancer weren't among them. One reason why these diseases have become epidemic is likely to be the diets people ate when they were young – the too-much-bad-fat, low vitamin syndrome.

Even more disturbing is the fact that our children's diets are becoming generally worse. Forty-odd years ago, fatty junk and convenience foods weren't around to the same degree. Now, kids are eating the same amount of meat and dairy their parents did when they were kids PLUS higher quantities of saturated fat, animal protein, sugar and salt. Today's children will almost certainly face even worse health statistics when they grow up than today's adults. And kids don't even have to 'grow up' before they get diseases once only seen in adulthood – obesity and type 2 diabetes are now increasingly afflicting teenagers.

Vegan kids are healthier

A vegan diet is very close to the official recommendations for healthy eating. But is it suitable for children? Of course it is. After the age of two, children should eat the same kinds of foods as their parents. Below that age, they need more fat and less fibre than adults. (See Viva!'s *Vegan New Parents' Guide* for information on bringing up vegan babies.)

Research studies show that vegan children obtain all the protein, energy and vitamins they need. It's true that it's necessary for vegans (small and big) to take vitamin D* and B12 supplements but if that's done, vegan children are better nourished than their peers.

A recent study revealed just how well vegan children fare – all of them had more than sufficient protein intake, ate more of healthy carbohydrates and fibre than non-vegan children but less sugar and their fat intake, including saturated fat, was lower (which is a good thing!) yet they had the highest intake of polyunsaturated 'good' fats (Alexy *et al.*, 2021). This study also showed that vegan children had the highest intake of vitamin E, vitamin C, folate, magnesium, iron and zinc among all children.

Other research shows that vegan children grow and develop at a normal rate, tend to be leaner (but within a healthy range) than their meat-eating counterparts and have a better quality diet (Melina *et al.*, 2016; Agnoli *et al.*, 2017; Baroni *et al.*, 2018, Lemale *et al.*, 2019).

As a result of their healthy diets, vegan children have a lower risk of developing obesity, diabetes and heart disease, some types of cancer, are less exposed to veterinary antibiotics (found in animal-based foods) and have lower levels of inflammation compared to meat-eating children (Melina *et al.*, 2016; Agnoli *et al.*, 2017; Ambroszkiewicz *et al.*, 2018; Baroni *et al.*, 2018, Lemale *et al.*, 2019).

And there's one more health perk to a vegan diet in childhood – eating this way helps children establish healthy, lifelong eating habits.

*Note everyone in the UK, adults and children, need to supplement vitamin D due to lack of sunlight, particularly in winter months.

Healthy Foods for Children

FRUIT AND VEG FOR KIDS
We all know it's important for children to eat plenty of fruit and veg every day. We know it but very few kids do it!

WHY FRUIT AND VEG?
All of us have 'free radicals' in our bodies and brains that run around like mad hooligans causing inflammation and disease such as heart disease, strokes, arthritis and cancer.

Fruit and veg contain 'antioxidants'. These are our health warriors, coming to our rescue. Antioxidants include beta-carotene (which makes vitamin A) and other carotenoids, vitamins C and E and flavonoids.

FLAVOURSOME FLAVONOIDS
Flavonoids are chemical compounds that plants produce to protect themselves from bacteria and damage to their cells. Flavonoids reduce

inflammation, boost the immune system and even aid memory and concentration. They can be helpful in treating attention-deficit hyperactivity disorder (ADHD) and other issues in children (Alvarez-Arellano *et al.*, 2020).

Over 4,000 flavonoids have been discovered so far and they are abundant in plants, including fruits and vegetables.

CRACKIN' CAROTENOIDS

There are over 500 carotenoids in plants – they are the pigments that make fruit and veg yellow, red, green and orange. The best-known is beta-carotene (which our bodies turn into vitamin A) – but all of them are protective including lycopene (plentiful in tomatoes and protective against some cancers), cryptoxanthin, lutein and zeaxanthin.

As you can see, plants contain thousands of natural chemicals that fight disease inside us. They also help to prevent disease happening in the first place. It's no good just popping a vitamin pill – they contain a fraction of the goodness that we get from eating fruit and veg, nuts, seeds and peas, beans and lentils.

WHAT IS A CHILD'S SERVING OF FRUIT AND VEGETABLES?

Children should eat at least five portions of a variety of fruit and vegetables a day. The amount of food a child needs varies with age, body size and physical activity. As a rough guide, one portion is the amount they can fit in the palm of their hand. Portion sizes increase gradually as children become older and more active. By the time children are 10, they should be eating the same size fruit and vegetable servings as adults.

5 A DAY for kids: How much do they need?

Children up to 10 years old need five portions of fruit and vegetables a day – their one portion is roughly the amount they can fit in the palm of their hand.

Older children should eat at least five servings and the following guidelines will give you an idea of portion sizes for teenagers and adults.

FRUIT PORTIONS

Fresh Fruit

- **Small-sized fruit** – One portion is two or more small fruits, for example: two plums, two satsumas, two kiwi fruit, three apricots, six lychees, seven strawberries or 14 cherries.
- **Medium-sized fruit** – One portion is one piece of fruit, such as one apple, banana, pear, orange or nectarine.
- **Large fruit** – One portion is half a grapefruit, one slice of papaya, one thick slice of melon (5 cm slice), one large slice of pineapple or two slices of mango (5 cm slices).

Dried fruit

A portion of dried fruit is around 30 grams. This is about one heaped tablespoon of raisins, currants or sultanas, one tablespoon of mixed fruit, two figs, three prunes or apricots or one handful of dried mango slices.

Tinned fruit

Whether in natural juice or syrup, tinned fruit contains too much sugar and has lost most of its goodness, so it doesn't count towards 5 A DAY.

VEGETABLE PORTIONS

Green vegetables
Two broccoli spears or four heaped tablespoons of kale, spinach, spring greens or green beans.

Cooked vegetables
Three heaped tablespoons of cooked vegetables, such as carrots, peas or sweetcorn, or five cauliflower or broccoli florets.

Salad vegetables
Three sticks of celery, a two-inch chunk of cucumber, one medium tomato or seven cherry tomatoes.

Tinned and frozen vegetables
Roughly the same quantity as you would eat for a fresh portion. However, while frozen vegetables are as good as fresh, tinned are usually not. There are some exceptions, such as peas or sweetcorn, that keep their nutritional value but with other veggies, you're best off buying fresh or frozen.

Potatoes
Potatoes don't count as vegetables. They do contain some important nutrients but not as many as other veggies – they mainly offer starchy carbohydrates. That means they are a good source of energy and in meals, they are typically used in place of other starchy foods, such as bread, rice or pasta. Potatoes have their place in a healthy diet, just not as vegetables.

Juices and Smoothies

One 150-millilitre glass of unsweetened 100 per cent fruit or vegetable juice can count as a portion. But only one glass counts, further glasses of juice don't count towards your total 5 A DAY portions.

One smoothie containing whole fruits and/or vegetables may count as more than one 5 A DAY portion if it's freshly made and contains either:

- at least 80 grams of one variety of whole fruit and/or vegetable and at least 80 grams of another variety of whole fruit and/or vegetable, or
- at least 80 grams of one variety of whole fruit and/or vegetable and at least 150 millilitres of a different variety of 100 per cent fruit and/or vegetable juice.

Smoothies count as a maximum of two of your 5 A DAY, however much you drink. It's because sugars are released from fruit when it's juiced or blended, and these sugars can contribute to tooth decay. Whole fruits are less likely to cause tooth decay because the sugars are contained within the structure of the fruit and are only released lower down in the digestive tract.

READY-MADE FOODS

Fruit and vegetables contained in shop-bought ready-made meals can also count toward your 5 A DAY, especially if they are fresh. Always read the label. Some ready-made foods contain high levels of fat, salt and sugar, so only have them occasionally or in small amounts as part of a healthy balanced diet.

Winning Tips for 5 A DAY for kids

TRY THESE QUICK TIPS

- Keep a bowl of fruit on the kitchen table for a quick, easy snack.
- Always have freshly cut vegetable sticks in the refrigerator.
- Add bananas and other fresh or dried fruits to hot or cold cereals.
- Buy frozen mixed berries. Defrost and add to your child's cereal or snacks daily.
- Top foods such as veggie sausages or burgers with a homemade salsa made with tomatoes, mangoes, avocados, red onions and lime juice.
- Add cut up fruit to pancakes.
- Provide dried fruit instead of sweets.
- Keep a variety of vegetables in the freezer and add them to stews, casseroles and stir-fried dishes.
- Freeze fruits such as bananas or grapes for a frozen treat.
- Whilst many kids won't eat a whole fruit, they devour chopped fruit in fruit salads – serve with a little plant-based ice cream.
- Always put fruit and veggies into your child's lunchbox.
- Use your imagination! A child who says 'Nah' to an apple may eat it if sliced thinly and fanned out. Make fruit faces or veggie monsters. Young children love this and will often reward your efforts by gobbling up the food and demanding more.
- Think rainbow. Get colour on your plates. Think of five colours, when you think about 5 A DAY for kids. It's what gives the fruit and veg their colour that also protects your child's health.
- Smoothies are a great way to add healthy foods to a child's diet without them thinking it's healthy! Try adding berries, banana and nut butter to plant milk and blend. Yum.

EMPOWER YOUR CHILD
- Let your child choose a fruit or vegetable that looks appealing at the supermarket.
- Involve your child in preparing meals so that he or she can become familiar with the foods.
- Have a raw and cooked vegetable option so that your child can choose the one they like best. Some children like the crunch in raw vegetables, while others like vegetables to be soft and mushy. Let them choose if they want one or both – just make sure they eat some!

DON'T GIVE UP
- Children can be very picky. It may take as many as 10 to 15 tries with a new food before a child is willing to accept it.
- Think about colour, smell and texture when introducing your child to a new food. A child may enjoy raw crunchy but not cooked broccoli, or soft roasted peppers but not freshly sliced raw peppers.
- Be a positive role model. Eat a variety of fruits and vegetables – eat what you want your child to eat.
- Encourage your child to try new foods in a comfortable meal environment and positive atmosphere.

BE A LITTLE SNEAKY
- Add broccoli florets or julienne carrots to pasta or potato salad.
- Add spinach, courgettes or kale to spaghetti sauce.
- Mash beans and add sweetcorn and carrots in veggie chilli.
- Use lots of vegetables and peas or lentils in puréed soups.
- Hide mashed carrots/swede/turnips in mashed potatoes.

Safety Note: Small pieces of fruits and vegetables, such as grapes and sweetcorn, may pose a choking hazard for children under four years of age. Cut grapes in quarters, mash peas or sweetcorn, grate carrots and remove strings from celery for younger children.

Recipe ideas

BUTTERFLY SANDWICH
- 1 slice wholemeal bread
- 2 tsp peanut butter
- ½ banana or 3 strawberries
- 1 celery stick

Spread the peanut butter on the bread and celery stick. Place banana or strawberry slices on the peanut butter. Cut the bread diagonally and arrange the triangle pieces so that the points touch each other in the middle. Place the celery stick between the two points on the triangle.

FROZEN FRUIT KEBABS
- Melons, pineapple, berries and grapes
- Skewers without sharp corners

Cut chunks of fresh fruits such as melons, pineapple, berries or grapes. Put the chunks on a stick without sharp corners and place inside the freezer until slightly frozen. These are great for an afternoon snack on a warm summer day.

STRAWBERRY AND BANANA KEBABS WITH CHOCOLATE
- Banana and strawberries

Slice banana and strawberries and put on a skewer. Add a little dark chocolate sauce (melt some dark chocolate). Simple and delicious!

ANTS ON A LOG
- 1 tbsp peanut or cashew butter
- 5 to 7 raisins
- 1 celery stick

Spread peanut butter into the celery stick. Place raisins on the peanut butter.

APPLE STRUDEL SLICES
- ½ apple
- 2 tsp of tahini
- 2 dried apricots

Slice the apple and spread some tahini on each slice. Chop the apricots in small pieces and sprinkle them on the apple slices.

Every nutrient a child needs and how to get it

All diets need to be properly planned – for vegans no more and no less than meat-eaters. All the foods you eat and their main nutrients – fat, carbohydrate, protein – provide calories. Calories mean energy and each food contains a certain amount of energy (calories).

ENERGY NEEDS

Recommended total daily calorie intakes (the lower number in each range is for the younger age and low level of physical activity, the higher number is for older age and increased physical activity):

1-3 years	1,000-1,400
4-6 years	1,200-1,800
7-10 years	1,200-2,200
11-14 years	1,600-2,800
15-18 years	1,800-3,200
Adults	1,800-3,000

CARBOHYDRATES

At least 50 per cent of all this energy should come from carbohydrates. For a girl aged 7-10 years that means 600-1,100 calories (about 150-275 grams of carbohydrates per day).

Carbohydrates are our main and most important source of energy. There are three types:

1. Fast-releasing, such as table sugar, white flour, sweets and syrups;
2. Slow-releasing complex carbohydrates, such as wholegrains (oats, wholegrain bread, brown rice, wholegrain pasta, rye), root vegetables, pulses;
3. Fibre – the indigestible component of fruits, vegetables, pulses and grains, essential for the digestive system to work properly.

In general, we should all be eating more slow-releasing carbohydrates than we do. A vegan diet – based on carbohydrate-rich plant foods – is the perfect way of doing that.

Two medium slices of wholemeal bread (about 75-90 g) contain 32-45 g of carbohydrate; a 50 g serving of breakfast cereal contains 45 g; 150 g serving of lentils (cooked) contains 30 g.

FIBRE

Adults are urged to eat 30 grams of fibre per day, yet the average intake is only about 18 grams! Children over two years of age should eat 15-20 grams daily, children over 10 should get 25 grams and older teenagers 30 grams.

Fibre is found only in plant foods and not in meat or dairy, so vegans tend to be well supplied. Fruits, vegetables, pulses and wholegrain bread, pasta, rice and oats provide it in abundance. Fibre is essential as it helps to prevent constipation, reduce cholesterol levels, makes us feel full (so helping to avoid overeating) and evens out blood sugar levels. It may also help to prevent some types of cancer.

½ a can of baked beans contains over 7 g of fibre; 200 g cooked wholewheat pasta 7 g; one medium apple has over 4 g.

PROTEIN

Daily intake – 14.5 grams (toddlers) to 55 grams (adults). About 15 per cent of our energy should come from protein, which is needed for growth, repairing the body and fighting infection – and there is more nonsense talked about it than any other nutrient.

Vegans get all they need simply by eating a variety of different foods – and it's healthier than animal protein. The bonus for vegans is that they also get more fibre and far less saturated fat.

Good sources of protein are pulses (peas, beans, lentils, chickpeas), nuts, seeds, wholegrain cereals and grains (bread, pasta, rice). Soya beans – in the form of soya milk, tofu (soya bean curd), tempeh, mock meats and soya sausages – are equivalent to meat in the amount and type of protein they provide. They also contain strong antioxidants (helping to protect our tissues from damage), essential fats, and are rich in fibre and phytoestrogens – natural chemicals that are thought to have anti-cancer properties (Messina, 2016; Applegate *et al.*, 2018).

Not only does soya contain no cholesterol, it can actually help lower cholesterol levels in the body! The large amount of evidence linking soya to good heart health has even led the US and UK to allow health claims to appear on certain food products containing soya (Jenkins *et al.*, 2019).

½ a can of baked beans contains 10 g of protein; 200 g of cooked wholewheat pasta has 12 g; 150 g cooked kidney beans 12 g; 28 g almonds (small handful) 6 g; one slice of wholemeal bread 4 g.

FAT FACTS

Fat should make up 30 to 40 per cent of your child's energy intake and up to 30 per cent of yours. Of this, no more than 10 per cent should be saturated fat, the remainder being a combination of monounsaturated and polyunsaturated fats (see definitions below).

Fats are essential for your cells, repairing body tissue, carrying some vitamins around the body and for manufacturing hormones. They also help lubricate our joints.

Fats are either saturated (mainly animal fats, coconut and palm oil) or unsaturated. You do not need to eat saturated fat but you do need some unsaturated fats – the so-called essential fatty acids or polyunsaturated fats.

There are two types – omega-3 and omega-6. Omega-3 fats are found in some nuts (especially walnuts), seeds (especially flaxseed, chia and hemp seeds) and soya beans – and oils exctracted from them – and dark green leafy vegetables such as broccoli. Omega-6 fats are found in seeds such as sunflower and sesame seeds, corn, some nuts (again walnuts) and soya beans and their oils. The most common oils available on the market – general vegetable oil blends – tend to be high in omega-6 fats but very low in omega-3 fats. Using only these types of oil may mean you miss out on the vital omega-3 fats.

Walnuts, flaxseed, hempseed and chia seeds are rich in both omega-3 and omega-6 fatty acids and in the right proportions that the body needs. Essential oils (especially omega-3 ones) are easily damaged by light or heat so they should be refrigerated and only used cold as dressings. That's why it's also best to refrigerate seeds and nuts.

A handful of walnuts, one or two tablespoons of the seeds listed above or a spoonful of their oils each day is enough to cover your body's needs. Rapeseed oil is also rich in omega-3s and is an exception because it is not degraded by heat so easily – making it a good choice for cooking.

Olive oil is a monounsaturated fat and a healthy choice if you want to top up your child's fat intake. There's also good evidence to suggest that olive oil, extra-virgin olive oil in particular, helps to lower your risk of heart disease and may be part of the reason why traditional Mediterranean diets are heart-healthy (Guasch-Ferré *et al.*, 2014).

And don't believe the hype surrounding oily fish as a necessary part of the diet for obtaining omega-3 fats. Most fish contain poisons such as mercury, dioxins and pesticide residues (Marcotrigiano and Storelli, 2003; Guéguen *et al.*, 2011; Bosch *et al.*, 2016; Savadatti *et al.*, 2019).

Fish get their omega-3s from certain types of algae, which are naturally rich in omega-3 fats. You can buy omega-3 vegan supplements made from algae, which are much healthier than fish, toxin-free and more sustainable.

1 slice of wholemeal bread contains 1.2 g of fat; ½ can of baked beans less than 1 g; a 28 g serving of almonds 14 g (most of which are good fats).

CALCIUM

Daily intake – 350 milligrams (toddlers) to 700 milligrams (adults). A milligram is a thousandth of a gram and may be written as mg.

Calcium is vital for healthy bones and teeth – in fact, almost our entire calcium supply is bound up in these tissues! Calcium is also involved in the working of many hormones, blood clotting, regulation of blood pressure, muscular contractions and the sending and receiving of nerve impulses.

Although dairy products contain calcium, cow's milk also contains unnecessary saturated fat and offers no fibre or other vital nutrients such as iron or vitamins C, E or beta-carotene.

Furthermore, as milk is taken from either a pregnant cow or a cow who has recently given birth, milk naturally contains 35 hormones, some of which have been linked to breast cancer (Grosvenor *et al.*, 1992; Ganmaa and Sato, 2005; Fraser *et al.*, 2020).

Despite all its marketing, drinking cow's milk is no guarantee of healthy bones (see Osteoporosis on page 68).

Vegan diets which include regular servings of dark green, leafy vegetables such as broccoli, kale, watercress and cabbage; tofu, beans, seeds (especially sesame and tahini – sesame seed paste) and nuts (especially almonds) are unlikely to be calcium deficient. Most plant milks are fortified with the same amount of calcium that cow's milk contains (around 240 mg in a 200 ml glass). So, making plant milk a regular part of your child's diet helps to top up their intake.

When you stop to think about it, drinking the milk of another species is a very strange thing to do, particularly when no animal has a need for it after weaning – and that includes humans. We do it out of habit and because it is heavily promoted. Imagine drinking the milk of your pet dog or an elephant. Sounds ludicrous – but no more so than drinking the milk of a cow!

"Ideally the infant should be exclusively fed human milk for the first year of life... After the first year of life the child requires no milk of any type. The child, like us adults, can thrive without cow milk ever crossing his lips."
Frank Oski MD, Formerly Specialist in Paediatric Nutrition and former Director, Department of Paediatrics, Johns Hopkins University School of Medicine and Physician-in-Chief, The Johns Hopkins Children's Centre

100 g tofu (brands vary) contains 200-500 mg calcium (make sure it is calcium-set); 1 slice wholemeal bread 58 mg; 100 g broccoli 40 mg; 28 g almonds 76 mg; 15 g serving (1 tbsp) of tahini (sesame seed paste) 64 mg; 100 ml of serving fortified plant milk 120 mg. This compares with 22 mg for a medium egg and 120 mg for cow's milk.

IODINE

Daily intake – 70 micrograms (toddlers) to 140 micrograms (adults).

Iodine is needed to produce thyroid hormones, that help to control metabolism and determine how fast you burn up food. In infants, thyroid hormones are responsible for development of the nervous system, including the brain.

Seaweed (arame, wakame and nori – hello sushi rolls!) and iodised salt are good sources. Kelp is very high in iodine so use only very sparingly. The following foods have varying iodine content depending on iodine levels in the soil in which they're grown: wholegrains, green beans, courgettes, kale, spring greens, watercress, strawberries and organic potatoes with skin. Amounts tend to be low and variable. An increasing number of plants milks also contain a source of iodine as potassium iodide – always check the ingredients!

If you're worried your child may not be getting enough iodine, there are iodine supplements made from kelp that contain safe amounts.

IRON

Daily intake – 6.9 milligrams (toddlers) to 14.8 milligrams (adults).

Iron helps red blood cells carry oxygen to all parts of the body and everyone needs a good supply. Leading health experts agree that iron deficiency anaemia is no more common in vegetarians than meat-eaters (Saunders *et al.*, 2013).

This is because there are plenty of iron sources in a vegan diet – pulses (beans, lentils, peas), tofu, tempeh, dark green leafy vegetables

(such as broccoli and kale), fortified breakfast cereals, wholegrains (such as wholemeal bread), dried apricots, prunes and figs, black treacle and even plain dark chocolate or cocoa.

The great thing about a vegan diet is that it is loaded with vitamin C from fresh fruits and vegetables which increases iron absorption (Melina *et al.*, 2016; Baroni *et al.*, 2018). Interestingly, we absorb more iron from soya (including tofu and tempeh) than from other plant sources (Agnoli *et al.*, 2017). Drinking tea can reduce iron absorption so avoid your cuppa an hour either side of eating iron-rich foods.

200 g of cooked lentils contains 7 mg of iron; ½ can of baked beans 3 mg; 2 slices wholemeal bread 3.5 mg; 50 g serving fortified breakfast cereal 3-6 mg.

Zinc

Daily intake – 5 milligrams (toddlers) to 9.5 milligrams (adults).

Zinc is involved in growth, the immune system (so helping to fight infection), wound healing and plays a crucial role in enzyme activity. Enzymes are chemicals which enable all the reactions that go on in the body (eg digestion of food) and zinc helps to keep these enzymes working properly.

Good sources include tofu, tempeh (fermented soya beans), wholewheat pasta, quinoa, brown rice, wheat germ, lentils, nutritional yeast, pumpkin seeds, cashew nuts, sesame seeds and tahini – sesame seed paste.

200 g of lentils contain 2.5 mg zinc; 200 g of wholewheat pasta 1.7 mg; 100 g of tofu 1.1 mg; 1 tbsp of pumpkin seeds 0.6 mg.

Vitamin A

Daily intake – 400 micrograms (toddlers) to 700 micrograms (adults). A microgram is a millionth of a gram and may be written as mcg.

Vitamin A is needed to maintain a healthy immune system, for the growth and development of tissues, for vision and healthy skin. There are two kinds – one found in plants, called beta-carotene, and one in meat called retinol. The body converts beta-carotene into vitamin A according to its needs and it also acts as an important antioxidant.

Animal vitamin A – retinol, found mostly in liver – is not an antioxidant and if taken in large quantities during pregnancy can cause birth defects. That's why plants are much better sources of vitamin A.

Foods rich in beta-carotene include carrots, pumpkins, butternut squash, sweet potatoes, peppers (red, yellow, orange), spinach, kale, watercress, romaine lettuce, tomatoes, mangoes, apricots and cantaloupe melon.

1 medium carrot contains 500 mcg of vitamin A, 1 tbsp of cooked spinach 118 mcg, ½ a red pepper 93 mcg, one medium tomato 51 mcg, three dried apricots 38 mcg.

B COMPLEX VITAMINS

B1 (THIAMINE)

Daily intake – 0.5 milligrams (toddlers) to 1.1 milligrams (adults).

Vitamin B1 helps to release energy from carbohydrates and fats, aids the functioning of the brain, heart and nerves and helps the body cope with stress. Good food sources include wholemeal bread, oats, brown rice, wholewheat pasta, breakfast cereals, sunflower and sesame seeds, wheatgerm, nutritional yeast, nuts (pecans, Brazil and hazelnuts) and pulses (lentils, beans, peas).

When wheat flour is refined to make white flour, thiamine is lost so white flour has to be fortified with it during manufacture. It's much better to buy wholemeal products that contain thiamine naturally!

1 slice of wholemeal bread contains 0.15 mg; 1 tbsp of sunflower seeds 0.13 mg; 1 tbsp of wheat germ 0.14 mg, 1 tsp of nutritional yeast 2.3 mg.

B2 (RIBOFLAVIN)

Daily intake – 0.6 milligrams (toddlers) to 1.3 milligrams (adults).

Riboflavin helps to release energy from fats, carbohydrates and protein and is important for healthy skin, hair and nails. It's widely available in plant foods such as nutritional yeast, wholegrains, fortified vegan breakfast cereals, almonds, avocado, kale, mushrooms and mangetout peas.

1 tsp of nutritional yeast contains 0.9 mg of riboflavin, 200 g of cooked brown rice 0.14 mg, 1 cup of oats (81 g) 0.13 mg, ½ an avocado 0.1 mg, 28 g of almonds 0.32 mg.

B3 (NiACiN)

Daily intake – eight milligrams (toddlers) to 18 milligrams (adults).

Niacin is needed to release energy from foods and for maintaining skin, nerve, brain and digestive health. It is found in nutritional yeast extract, wholegrains including wholemeal bread, fortified vegan breakfast cereals, quinoa, muesli, brown rice, wild rice, wholemeal spaghetti, peanuts and peanut butter, corn on the cob, peas and sunflower seeds.

1 tsp of nutritional yeast contains 17 mg of niacin, 200g wholewheat pasta contains 6.25 mg niacin; 1 slice of wholemeal bread 1.9 mg; 1 tbsp peanut butter 2.3 mg.

B6 (Pyridoxine)

Daily intakes – 0.7 milligrams (toddlers) to 1.5 milligrams (adults).

Vitamin B6 is needed for breaking down protein, producing red blood cells and absorbing zinc. It is easily obtained from wholegrains, fortified vegan breakfast cereals, wheatgerm, nutritional yeast, avocados, bananas, prunes, beans, dried fruits, seeds and nuts.

1 medium banana contains 0.43 mg of vitamin B6; ½ an avocado 0.24 mg; 1 tsp of nutritional yeast 1.7 mg, 1 tbsp of sunflower seeds 0.12 mg.

B9 (Folate or Folic Acid)

Daily intakes – 70 micrograms (toddlers) to 200 micrograms (everyone over 11).

Folate helps with the making of red blood cells, forming DNA (your genetic blueprint), is important for brain and nerve function, and is vital in preventing defects in the developing foetus. It is plentiful in a healthy vegan diet, in foods such as green vegetables (asparagus, Brussel's sprouts, spinach, kale, white cabbage, pak choi, rocket, broccoli, lettuce and peas), soya and products made from it (edamame, tempeh, tofu), lentils, nutritional yeast, hazelnuts, oranges, tomatoes, red peppers and sweetcorn.

100 g cooked broccoli contains 105 mcg of folate, 10 hazelnuts 16 mcg; 100 g cooked lentils 180 mcg.

B12 (COBALAMIN)

Daily intakes – five micrograms (toddlers) to 50 micrograms (everyone over 11).

Vitamin B12 is essential for a healthy nervous system, blood formation, DNA production and helps us to use energy from food. Your liver has stores that can cover your needs for up to three years but you need a regular intake. Once a deficiency develops, it can cause serious nerve damage.

Vitamin B12 is made by bacteria in the soil and water. Traditionally, people, as well as animals, got it naturally by eating foods from the ground with those B12-producing bacteria stuck to them. However, food production systems are now very different, everything is washed and cleaned, and some plant foods are not even grown in real soil! That's why we need to take a supplement. Animal products contain vitamin B12 because the animals are given this vitamin in their feed too.

Plant foods don't contain vitamin B12 in reliable quantities, except for B12 fortified foods, such as plant milks, yoghurts, cereal products and margarine. Even these foods may not provide enough, so everyone needs a supplement to make sure we get our daily dose.

Experts (Agnoli *et al.*, 2017; Baroni *et al.*, 2018) recommend these daily doses taken in the supplement form: 5 mcg for children up to three years of age, 25 mcg for children from four to 10, and 50 mcg daily for older children and adults.

Vitamins B6, B12 and folate help keep the heart healthy by lowering levels of a chemical in the body called homocysteine. High levels of homocysteine have been linked to increased risk for heart disease and strokes so it is vital that adequate amounts of these B-vitamins are supplied daily in the diet.

VITAMIN C (ASCORBIC ACID)

Daily intakes – 30 milligrams (toddlers) to 40 milligrams (everyone over 15).

Your body can't store vitamin C so it needs to be eaten every day. It's an important vitamin – involved in wound healing, maintaining healthy skin, blood vessels and healthy gums. It is also an important antioxidant, helping to keep the immune system fighting fit. And lastly, vitamin C helps the body absorb iron.

It is present in a wide range of plant foods but there is none in animal products. Rich sources are berry fruits such as blackcurrants and strawberries, citrus fruits such as oranges as well as pineapple, mango, green leafy vegetables (eg broccoli), kiwi fruits and tomatoes. Potatoes contain some vitamin C and are an important source, particularly in winter.

½ of an orange contains 35 mg of vitamin C, 1 kiwi fruit 64 mg, 100 g of cooked broccoli 65 mg, 6 cherry tomatoes 14 mg.

VITAMIN D

Daily intake – 8.5 micrograms for babies up to the age of one year, 10 micrograms for everyone over the age of one year.

Vitamin D is necessary for the regulation of calcium and phosphate levels in the body. It is needed for strong bones and teeth, and for a healthy immune system.

The main source of vitamin D is your skin – when exposed to sunlight, the UV portion of the light triggers vitamin D production from molecules already present in your skin.

In the UK, from April to October, we get most of our vitamin D from sunlight exposure. On a sunny day, you can make all the vitamin D you need by exposing your face, arms and legs for 10 to 40 minutes twice a week. If you are fair-skinned, 15 minutes might be all you need. The darker your skin, the more sunlight exposure you need – if your skin is very dark, you may need the full 40 minutes to produce enough vitamin D.

Sunscreen blocks vitamin D production and so does glass and fabric – if you always protect your child's skin, they may not be getting enough vitamin D even in the summer.

When it comes to the colder months – October to April – there's just not enough sunlight during the day and it's too weak, even on a sunny day, so it's recommended that we all take a supplement.

All babies up to 12 months of age should be given vitamin D drops. Toddlers and older children preferably too as we usually protect their skin, so it may not be able to make enough – they should get a supplement at least from October to April if not throughout the whole year (Amit, 2010; Baroni *et al.*, 2018). The recommended dose is the same for everyone – 10 micrograms daily – in babies up to 12 months it is 8.5-10 micrograms.

VITAMIN E (TOCOPHEROL)

Daily intake – six milligrams (toddlers) to 15 milligrams (adults).

Vitamin E is a powerful antioxidant that protects cells from damage, maintains healthy skin and supports the immune system. It also reduces the risk of blood clots – protecting against heart disease and strokes. Only found in plant foods, rich sources are vegetable oils, nuts and seeds (hazelnuts, almonds, sunflower seeds, peanuts, peanut butter and pistachios), avocado, butternut squash, canned tomatoes, broccoli, spinach, kale, mango and wheatgerm.

1 tbsp of sunflower seeds contains 3 mg of vitamin E, 1 tbsp of peanut butter 1.5 mg, ½ an avocado 4 mg, 1 tbsp of wheatgerm 1.6 mg.

Vegan eatwell plate for children

- 3-5 portions of wholegrains
- 5-8 portions of fruit and vegetables
- 3-4 portions of pulses, nuts and seeds
- + Vitamin B12 and D supplements
- + Small amounts of treats
- 1-2 portions of essential healthy fats
- + Water: 1-2 litres daily

*For healthy portion sizes see pages 14 and 15

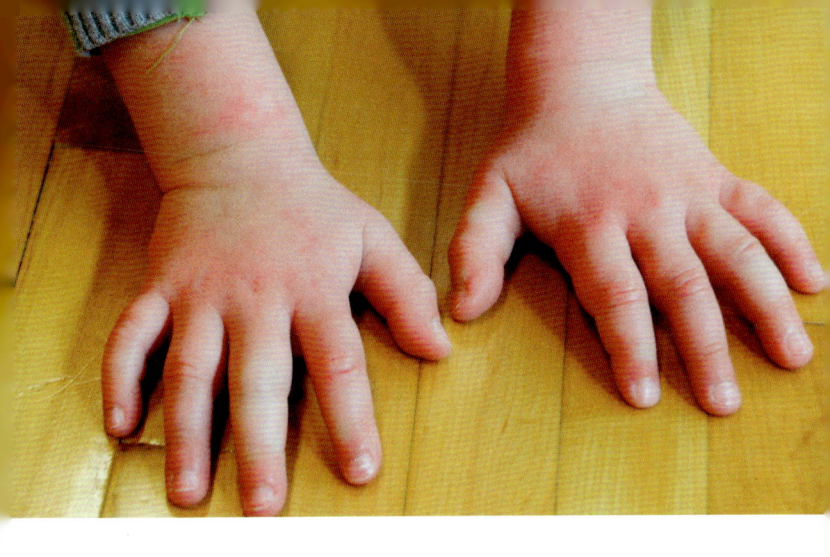

How animal products affect children

ALLERGIES

The word allergy describes a bad reaction to something – it is the body's defence (immune) system leaping to protect you against what it believes is a foreign invader. Asthma (breathlessness with wheezing), eczema (red, itchy and flaky skin), rhinitis (constant runny or congested nose), hay fever and urticaria (skin rashes) are classical allergies. Usually, this defence reaction is unnecessary and so allergies are an overreaction of your immune system – it can be something you're born with but also a temporary sign that your body isn't functioning 100 per cent as it should.

Reactions can be particularly violent – and deadly – with allergies to foods such as peanuts. On the other hand, food intolerance is not the same as allergy and produces a less dramatic and slower reaction.

The most common food allergies are to cow's milk, eggs, shellfish, fish, nuts and peanuts, wheat and soya. A reaction to the main protein in cow's milk (casein) is the most common allergy in childhood. When a baby swallows cow's milk, bits of this protein get into his or her immune system and can trigger a reaction. Excessive mucus production resulting in a constant runny nose, blocked ears or a persistent sore throat are often the first signs of a problem with cow's milk. More serious problems such as eczema, colic, diarrhoea, asthma and vomiting are the body's way of trying to get rid of the invader. In fact, research discovered a link between cow's milk allergy and asthma so by avoiding dairy products, susceptible children may also be avoiding the risk of asthma (Jansen *et al.*, 2018).

CROHN'S DISEASE

Crohn's disease is a debilitating, chronic (long-term) inflammation of the digestive system that is incurable. Once it develops, it requires a very specific diet and can cause many complications.

It's linked to meat and dairy foods through the MAP bacterium (*Mycobacterium avium subspecies paratuberculosis*) that causes Johne's disease in cattle. MAP infection is widespread among cattle and the bacteria are commonly found in commercial milk (it survives pasteurisation) and in beef (Naser *et al.*, 2014). That means you can get infected by consuming milk or beef but also by inhaling MAP in fine water spray from rivers contaminated with cow manure. The infection doesn't cause Crohn's in everyone but if you have a certain genetic make-up that makes you susceptible, MAP may trigger the disease (Naser *et al.*, 2014).

HEART DISEASE

Coronary heart disease, or CHD, results from the narrowing of the main blood vessels around the heart – coronary arteries – which is why it's also called coronary artery disease. The problem stems from hard fatty deposits of cholesterol stiffening and clogging up the arteries – atherosclerosis. Blood supply to the heart muscles is reduced and may eventually stop completely and the result is a heart attack.

Cholesterol is a major risk factor for CHD – the more saturated fat we eat, the more cholesterol the body produces. Saturated fat is mostly found in animal products (meat, dairy and eggs) but also in coconut and palm oil. Sadly, a lot of children's foods are stacked with saturated fat.

Research revealed that children as young as three years may already have fatty patches in their blood vessels. As these children are growing up, the fatty patches develop into atherosclerotic plaques, which is why people in their early twenties can have extensive atherosclerosis (Desmond *et al.*, 2018).

Children fed unhealthy diets full of meat, fat and sugar are more likely to have higher cholesterol, fat and sugar levels in their blood and higher than healthy body weight (Shang *et al.*, 2020). On the other hand, healthy childhood diets not only lower heart disease risk in adulthood but vegan children also have lower cholesterol levels and more antioxidants in the blood – this helps to protect their blood vessels and hearts even more (Desmond *et al.*, 2018 and 2021; Alexy *et al.*, 2021).

DENTAL HEALTH

You don't need telling that sugar is enemy number one when it comes to tooth decay (dental caries). But all kinds of foods can play a part, depending on their stickiness and nutrient content. A small plain chocolate bar eaten in one go for instance is less damaging than sucking on a chewy sweet that literally sticks to the teeth and remains there for ages.

When it comes to sugar and starchy foods that release sugars quickly – cornflakes, potato crisps, processed snacks – those are always bad news for the teeth. On the other hand, unrefined starchy foods such as wholegrains, pulses, fruit and vegetables (that also contain natural sugars) don't increase the risk of tooth decay (Halvorsrud *et al.*, 2019).

When your child eats or drinks something sweet or acidic, try to make them have a few sips of plain water afterwards to wash the food/drink remnants off their teeth.

DIABETES

Type 1 diabetes is when the body produces too little or no insulin and usually develops in childhood. Type 2 is when insulin is still produced but the body becomes insensitive to it and usually develops later in life.

Insulin is a hormone which makes it possible for cells to absorb glucose (sugar) from the blood. Without it, blood sugar levels rise and cells don't have enough energy. Diabetes can lead to heart disease, kidney failure and blindness.

When babies and young children with a specific genetic make-up are given cow's milk, it may accidentally trigger type 1 diabetes by destroying the body's ability to produce insulin in the pancreas (Chia *et al.*, 2017). For more information, see viva.org.uk/health/diabetes.

With type 2 diabetes, the situation is different. Unhealthy diets are a major risk factor with research showing that a bad diet in childhood increases the risk of type 2 diabetes in later teenage years and adulthood (Desmond *et al.*, 2018). What makes things worse is that when type 2 diabetes develops in adolescents, it progresses faster than in adults, leading to other health issues (Serbis *et al.*, 2021).

The good news is that a wholesome vegan diet can prevent this from happening – in fact, vegans have up to 50 per cent lower risk of type 2 diabetes (Appleby and Key, 2016; Salas-Salvadó *et al.*, 2019).

FOOD POISONING

A recent government report revealed that an astonishing 2.4 million people in the UK get food poisoning each year (FSA, 2020). It means that bacteria or viruses present in the food cause an infection with a range of unpleasant symptoms, usually including vomiting and diarrhoea. The youngest and the oldest are the most vulnerable and at risk of severe symptoms, such as dehydration, kidney failure and in extreme cases even death.

Eating animal products is behind most cases of food poisoning – in particular poultry, red meat, dairy, seafood and eggs (Lund, 2015). Plant foods can be contaminated too (often by animal waste) but if you're vegan, your risk is much lower.

According to the Food Standards Agency's research (FSA, 2020), the main pathogens causing most cases of food poisoning are norovirus, *Campylobacter*, *Salmonella* and *Clostridium perfringens*.

Perhaps even more worrying is the fact that many bacteria, including some of those that cause food poisoning, are antibiotic-resistant (also called superbugs). Antibiotics are the last refuge when food poisoning develops into blood poisoning. There are now fewer and fewer that will work when they're really needed – to save lives. Antibiotics have been systematically overused in animal farming in a desperate attempt to control the rampant diseases that spread at farms and many bacteria have simply become resistant.

Despite efforts to reduce antibiotic overuse in farming systems, the number of antibiotic-resistant bloodstream infections in the UK increased by 35 per cent between 2013-2017 and continues to rise (PHE, 2019).

Eating no animal products not only cuts your and your child's risk of food poisoning, it also reduces the need for antibiotic use in farming and thus reduces the development of antibiotic-resistant bacteria.

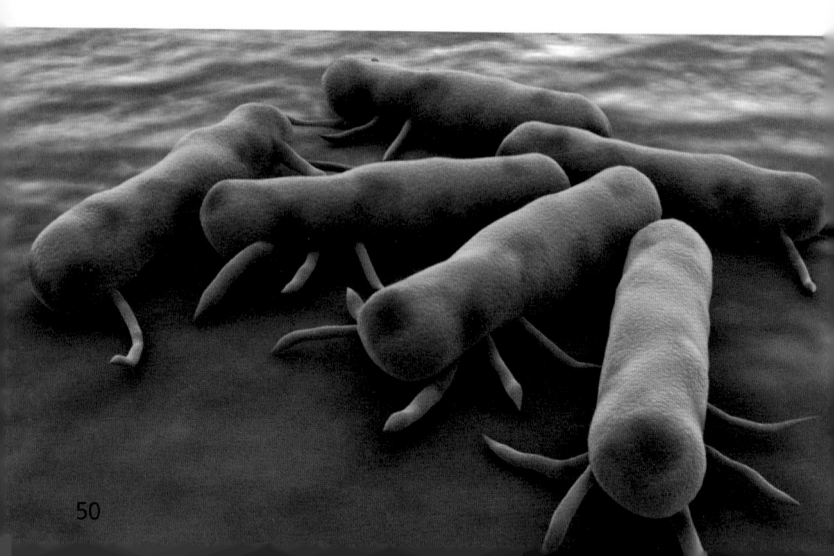

OVERWEIGHT AND OBESITY

The UK population as a whole has a serious weight problem and that includes children. In England, 23 per cent of 4-5-year-olds are overweight or obese, while by the age 10-11, this figure rises to 34 per cent (NHS, 2020).

Scientific studies show that children who are obese are more likely to become obese adults too (Simmonds *et al.*, 2015; Desmond *et al.*, 2018). And while in children, obesity brings an increased risk of high blood pressure, type 2 diabetes and breathing problems, in adulthood, it also increases the risk of heart disease, some types of cancer and infections.

There's no mystery about the causes of obesity – diet and physical activity play equal parts. Meat and dairy (such as cheese, butter and ice cream) come loaded with hefty amounts of saturated fats while sugary and processed foods supply large amounts of sugar and unhealthy fats. A lack of healthy foods, such as fruit and vegetables, beans or nuts also plays a major role.

Vegan diets usually provide more fruit and veggies, wholegrains, pulses, nuts and seeds – foods associated with healthy weight management. Vegan and vegetarian children tend to be within healthy weight ranges and have lower rates of obesity which gives them a healthy start to life (Desmond *et al.*, 2018 and 2021).

RHEUMATOID ARTHRITIS

Rheumatoid arthritis affects hundreds of thousands of adults, usually at older age, but it can also develop in children – about one in a 1,000 children has it. It's an inflammatory condition causing joint pain, stiffness and swelling and there's no known cure.

However, it can be managed through diet, favouring anti-inflammatory foods over those that can cause flare-ups. The Arthritis

Foundation recommend a diet rich in dark green leafy vegetables, berries, nuts and seeds, healthy fats including omega-3s, wholegrains, beans, lentils and onions (Arthritis Foundation, 2021). On the other hand, they suggest avoiding processed foods, microwaveable meals, fried foods, white flour products (bread, cakes, doughnuts, biscuits), red meat, sweets, fizzy drinks, sugary snacks and cereals, and crisps.

In some cases, a food intolerance can be a trigger or make matters worse – as milk is the most common troublemaker, cutting out dairy may also help children who suffer from arthritis.

TOXINS

Government tests show that more than 40 per cent of all our food contains pesticide residues (DEFRA, 2020).

Highly poisonous chemicals have polluted all the world's oceans and they have contaminated every single sea creature (Bosch *et al.*, 2016). Because of this, eating fish is increasingly a risky business – and particularly oily fish such as mackerel, herring, sprats and pilchards because fat soaks up the poisons. Farmed salmon, who are largely fed on wild-caught fish, are a particular problem.

The culprits are toxic heavy metals such as lead, cadmium, arsenic and mercury, and substances called PCBs and dioxins – these can damage the immune system and affect a child's intelligence. They may even disrupt the hormone balance in the body, affecting the development of reproductive organs and gender identity. Produced by industrial processes, PCBs are now banned but they will hang around in the environment for decades. As for other pollutants and heavy metals, there are officially-set limits to what's acceptable but no one measures them in every single fish product.

The problem of dioxins and PCBs accumulating in fatty foods, such as meat, dairy and fatty fish, is serious as these foods are responsible for 95 per cent of human exposure to these dangerous chemicals (Zennegg, 2018). By feeding your child vegan food, you are protecting them from substantial doses of these toxins.

Viva! Health resources

- Find out all the essential information about diet and your health in our **A-Z of Foods, A-Z of Nutrients, A-Z of Diseases** and more! See: viva.org.uk/health/a-zs
- For more information on **Children's Nutrition and Health**, go to: viva.org.uk/children
- If you're active, our **Vegan Sports Nutrition** pages are the right place for you: viva.org.uk/sports
- To learn about **Bone Health** and how to protect is, go to: viva.org.uk/bones
- Find out how to **Defeat Diabetes with Diet** at: viva.org.uk/diabetes
- Read all the important information on preventing and treating **Heart Disease** at: viva.org.uk/heart-health
- For all must-know information on vegan diets and health see our guide *Vegan for Health*: viva.org.uk/vegan-health-guide
- And for more in-depth details on your health and various health conditions, see *The Incredible Vegan Health Report*: viva.org.uk/vegan-health-report

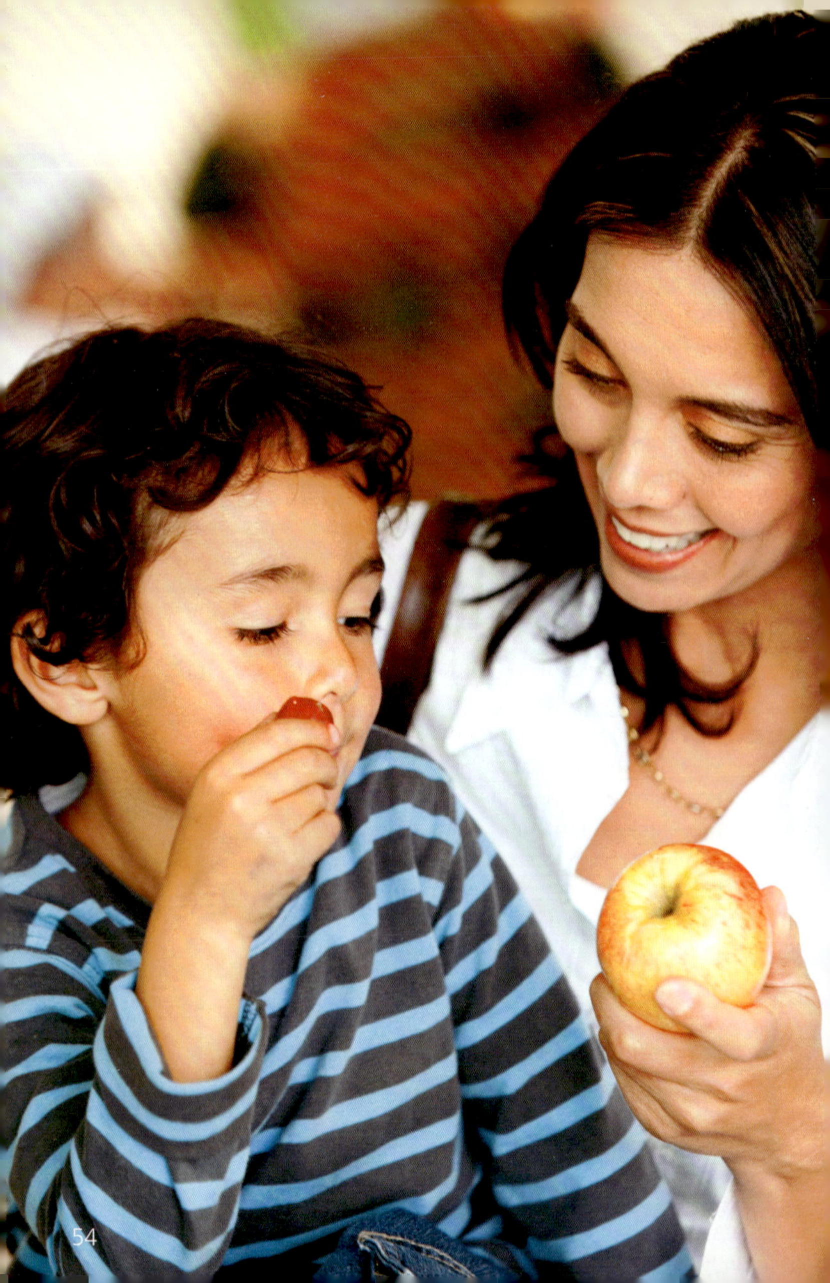

How animal products affect adults

Little people inevitably become big people so it's important to look at how animal products can affect adult health. Globally, one in five deaths is associated with poor diet – usually characterised by a lack of healthy foods, such as wholegrains, fruit, nuts and seeds, and too much processed food, meat and high-fat products (GBD 2017 Diet Collaborators, 2019). Children who learn healthy eating habits tend to eat healthily when they grow up too so a plant-based diet has long-term importance for them – but also for parents!

CANCER

In the UK, around a thousand people are diagnosed with cancer every day and these rates are one of the highest in the world (CRUK, 2020).

Cancer experts know that many cancer cases are preventable – between 30 and 50 per cent of all cancer cases could be avoided if people ate better, quit smoking, exercised more and reduced environmental pollution (WCRF, 2018).

The World Cancer Research Fund's comprehensive report (2018) highlights that to reduce your risk of cancer, you should eat a diet rich in wholegrains, fruit, vegetables and beans, limit your consumption of junk food and processed foods high in fat and/or sugar, severely cut down red and processed meat consumption, and limit fizzy drinks and alcohol.

A large-scale review of data on nutrition and cancer risk in childhood and adulthood concluded that the biggest diet-related risk factors are obesity and a diet high in meat, especially processed meat, fat, salt and alcohol (Mosby *et al.*, 2012). On the other hand, the study revealed that people consuming a plant-based diet have a much lower risk of cancer. These results have been supported by many other studies, most notably a large study from Oxford University which found that British vegans have a one fifth lower risk of cancer than meat-eaters (Key *et al.*, 2014). The results of the US Adventist Health Study II (AHS-2) were similar, revealing that vegans had a 16 per cent lower risk of all cancers combined (Tantamango-Bartley *et al.*, 2013) and other scientific studies show 15-18 per cent lower cancer rates in vegans (Huang *et al.*, 2012; Dinu *et al.*, 2017; Segovia-Siapco and Sabaté, 2019).

Meat has been repeatedly linked to cancer and many experts would like to see health warnings on meat products. In 2015, the World Health Organisation (WHO) classified processed meat as carcinogenic (causing cancer) and red meat as probably carcinogenic (Bouvard *et al.*, 2015). Even small amounts of red and processed meat have been shown to increase the risk of colon, breast and prostate cancer (Wolk, 2017).

For more information, see Viva!'s report *Meat the Truth*.

BREAST CANCER

Some 55,200 new breast cancer cases are diagnosed in the UK every year – it's the most common type of cancer in Britain and one in seven women will be diagnosed with it in their lifetime (CRUK, 2020).

Asian countries traditionally have much lower rates of breast cancer but with the rising popularity of Western foods, breast cancer rates have been creeping up. A large study of almost 50,000 Japanese women spanning over 15 years found that women eating traditional diets that are low in meat, dairy, processed foods and fatty condiments, such as mayo, have much lower rates of breast cancer compared to Japanese women eating Western-style diet rich in these products (Shin *et al.*, 2016). In fact, the study showed that, on average, favouring Western diets increased the risk of breast cancer by 32 per cent and in women whose diets were almost entirely based on these foods, the risk rose to 83 per cent!

Authors of a major review on the effect of foods on breast cancer risk revealed that the worst offenders were red and processed meats, sugary and processed foods, eggs and some dairy products (Buja *et al.*, 2020).

While there's plenty of scientific data showing how meat increases the risk of cancer, when it comes to breast cancer, milk can also make matters worse. It's because of a hormone called Insulin-like growth factor 1 (IGF-1). The same hormone occurs naturally in humans and stimulates growth in children but declines as a child ages. However, in an adult body, it can stimulate the growth of cancer cells. Not only is there IGF-1 in cow's milk but its consumption also stimulates your own body to produce more of it – a double whammy!

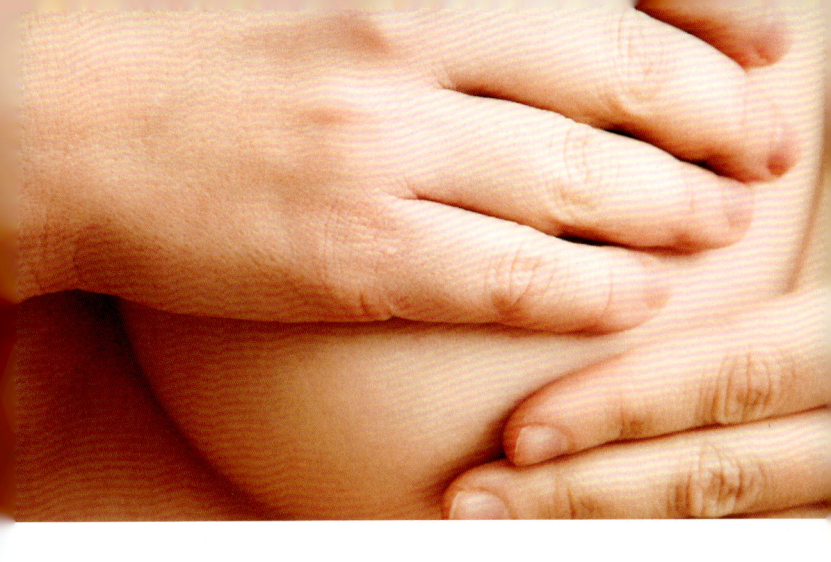

In a large-scale North American study, it was discovered that women consuming cow's milk have higher levels of IGF-1 compared to women consuming soya milk (Fraser *et al.*, 2020). And a European study found virtually the same results (Romo Ventura *et al.*, 2020). Vegans, on the other hand, have been found to have significantly lower levels of IGF-1 than people consuming dairy and meat (Allen *et al.*, 2002; McCarty, 2014).

BOWEL CANCER

Over 43,200 people develop cancer of the colon and rectum each year in the UK – around 110 are diagnosed every day (CRUK, 2020).

Bowel cancer is tightly linked to diet and lifestyle with red and processed meat consumption being the main culprit. According to a study performed by a group of top cancer experts, eating 100 grams of red meat (beef, pork, lamb, veal, mutton and goat) a day increases your bowel cancer risk by 17 per cent, while just 50 grams of processed meat (ham, sausages, salami, bacon) daily increases it by 18 per cent (Bouvard *et al.*, 2015).

When you eat hardly any fruit and vegetables, have low fibre intake but eat plenty of meat, you create the perfect storm for bowel cancer to occur (O'Keefe, 2016). It's not only about cancer-causing compounds in meat, it's also about what happens to the food in your gut.

High meat and fat consumption encourages certain species of gut bacteria to thrive and those are the bad ones – producing harmful by-products and making your gut wall inflamed, making it more vulnerable to damage and potential cancer growth (O'Keefe, 2016). On the other hand, when you eat plant wholefoods, the fibre they provide feeds the good bacteria in your gut that produce health-protective by-products and lower inflammation.

Many studies show how important fibre is in the prevention of bowel cancer. The largest European nutrition and health study (EPIC study) discovered that there is a 13 per cent decrease in the risk of colorectal cancer for each 10 grams of fibre consumed from plant wholefoods (Murphy *et al.*, 2012).

Add to it the many beneficial phytonutrients plants provide that actively help to protect your cells and you'll see why a plant-based diet can offer a substantial degree of protection from bowel cancer!

PROSTATE CANCER

Prostate cancer is the most common cancer in men with around 130 new cases being diagnosed every day in the UK (CRUK, 2020).

As with other types of cancer, meat – especially red and processed meat – consumption increases your chances of developing the disease but studies show that higher fat and dairy milk consumption also pose a risk (Mandair *et al.*, 2014).

The reason why dairy products have been linked to prostate cancer is the hormone IGF-1 – the same as in breast cancer – but also the hormone oestrogen, naturally present in all cow's milk (Sargsyan and Dubasi, 2021). There's been much debate about why milk increases the risk of prostate cancer and while several mechanisms are possible, it's not yet clear which is the main one.

What is clear, however, is that vegans have a 35 per cent lower risk of prostate cancer (Tantamango-Bartley *et al.*, 2016). A recent study revealed that a healthy vegan diet has many positive health effects that all work together in lowering the prostate cancer risk (McCarty, 2017).

the very best anti-cancer diet

According to Oxford scientists who conducted a thorough analysis, the key components to a cancer-risk lowering diet are fibre-rich foods (all plant wholefoods), fruit and vegetables, limiting or avoiding alcohol consumption, avoiding processed and junk foods linked to obesity and foods preserved by salting, such as some fish (Key *et al.*, 2020).

The World Cancer Research Fund (2018) state:

"One of our Cancer Prevention Recommendations is to make wholegrains, vegetables, fruit, and pulses (legumes) such as beans and lentils a major part of your usual daily diet. There is evidence that eating wholegrains, fibre, vegetables and fruit can help protect against certain cancers, as well as against weight gain, overweight and obesity."

In a nutshell, a healthy vegan diet ticks all the boxes to be the best anti-cancer diet! However, even the best diet won't make you cancer-proof because there are other factors at play. A wholesome diet can simply reduce your risk, while an unhealthy diet can increase it.

There are several foods that offer an extra bit of protection, including cruciferous vegetables (broccoli, cabbage, radish, watercress, rocket) – they contain substantial amounts of glucosinolates; substances that actively boost your body's defences against cancer (Bosetti *et al.* 2012; Abdull Razis and Noor, 2013).

Plant foods also contain protective 'plant hormones' – phytoestrogens – and soya is the best source. Despite earlier controversies that stemmed from flawed animal studies, research shows overwhelmingly beneficial effects of regular soya consumption – it can lower the risk of breast, lung, stomach, bowel and possibly even prostate cancer (Rizzo and Baroni, 2018).

Most plant wholefoods contain a variety of phenolic compounds that act as antioxidants and have been shown to have strong anti-cancer properties (Sharma *et al.*, 2018). The richer the colour, the more of these compounds plants tend to contain. On the other hand, animal products contain none.

A vegan diet is naturally bursting with many nutrients that protect us against cancer while an animal-based diet contains many potentially cancer-causing compounds. If your care about your health, the message is clear – go vegan to slash your risk of cancer!

CORONARY HEART DISEASE (CHD)

It is estimated that more than a half of the UK population will develop a heart or circulatory (blood vessel) disease in their lifetime and someone dies because of it every three minutes (BHF, 2021). Heart disease as such is the leading cause of premature death in the UK and someone dies of it every eight minutes.

Yet heart disease is among the top diseases that are not just preventable but also reversible with diet and lifestyle modifications. As Dr. Kim Williams, the former president of the American College of Cardiology famously said: "There are two kinds of cardiologists: vegans and those who haven't read the data."

Vegans and people who eat predominantly wholefood plant-based diets have consistently lower blood pressure and cholesterol levels than all other diet groups and a much lower risk of heart disease – 25-57 per cent (Bradbury *et al.*, 2014; Le and Sabaté, 2014; Appleby and Key, 2016; Dinu *et al.*, 2017; Benatar and Stewart, 2018; Kahleova *et al.*, 2018; Korakas *et al.*, 2018; Matsumoto *et al.*, 2019).

Cholesterol is a major player in the development of CHD. There's 'good' cholesterol and 'bad' cholesterol – bad cholesterol (low-density lipoproteins or LDL) is dumped on the artery walls, narrowing them and reducing blood flow. Eventually, these cholesterol deposits can cause heart attacks and strokes. Good cholesterol (high-density lipoproteins or HDL) is carried to the liver so the body can get rid of it.

To lower your cholesterol levels and keep them down, it's crucial to reduce your saturated fat intake – saturated fat is found mostly in meat, dairy, eggs, coconut and palm oil.

Compared to meat-eaters, vegans have a 63 per cent lower risk of high blood pressure – another major risk factor for heart disease (Pettersen *et al.*, 2012). If you already suffer from it, a healthy vegan diet can help you lower your blood pressure more effectively than a vegetarian one (Lee *et al.*, 2020).

Even if you have heart disease, a wholesome vegan diet can dramatically improve your health, reduce the need for medication and may even reverse the condition (Esselstyn *et al.*, 2014). In fact, a wholefood plant-based diet is the only diet that has been able to reverse heart disease (Kahleova *et al.*, 2018).

Plant-based diets have such a positive effect on our heart health because they contain less saturated fat, no cholesterol, plenty of fibre and many beneficial phytochemicals that actively help to make your blood vessels and heart healthier, and can reduce cholesterol plaques in your arteries.

And there's another reason why a plant-based diet protects your heart – research suggests that vegetarians naturally have more salicylic acid in the blood – some had levels 12 times higher than meat-eaters (Blacklock *et al.*, 2001). Salicylic acid is the main ingredient in aspirin, prescribed to reduce the risk of heart attacks by fighting the inflammation that causes it. Salicylic acid is also naturally present in fruit and vegetables which explains the higher levels in people who eat mostly plants.

DIABETES

Diabetes type 2 is much more common than type 1. In the UK, there are over 4.7 million people living with diabetes and the number has more than doubled over the last 20 years (Diabetes UK, 2019). In

England, over 10 million people are at an increased risk of developing type 2 diabetes.

Science shows that vegans have up to 50 per cent lower risk of type 2 diabetes (Appleby and Key, 2016; Salas-Salvadó et al., 2019). It's partly due to the healthier diets with plenty of fibre and fresh produce and also because they tend to be leaner – obesity is a major risk factor for type 2 diabetes.

Even if you already have type 2 diabetes, there's good news – a healthy vegan diet low in fat and high in wholefoods can help reverse it (Barnard et al., 2009; Kahleova et al., 2011; McMacken and Shah, 2017). In several studies, many patients were able to reduce their diabetes medication after several weeks of a wholefood plant-based diet and some were even able to discontinue it because they were no longer diabetic!

DIVERTICULAR DISEASE

Diverticular disease is one of the most common disorders of the colon among elderly people in Western societies. It develops when small pouches form in the gut wall and become inflamed, causing pain, nausea, fever and digestive problems.

Plant-based diets have proved very useful in the prevention of this disease. For example, the long-running EPIC Oxford study revealed that vegetarians had a 31 per cent lower risk of diverticular disease compared with meat-eaters (Crowe et al., 2011). Fibre intake is particularly important in the prevention of diverticular disease – in this study, people with the highest fibre intakes (more than 26 grams a day) had a 41 per cent lower risk.

And another recent study found that in an Asian population, non-vegetarian diet increased the risk of diverticular disease by a huge 80 per cent (Bong et al., 2020)!

GALLSTONES

Gallstones are made up mostly of cholesterol crystals and are formed when bile (digestive fluid) becomes saturated with cholesterol. The causes are the same old suspects – too little fibre, high saturated fat intake, too much processed and sugary foods, high cholesterol and obesity (Gaby, 2009). A vegan diet can lower the risk, especially if it's high in fibre. In one study, a vegetarian diet lowered the risk of gallstones in women by 48 per cent (Chang *et al.*, 2019).

Hypertension

High blood pressure is caused by stress, alcohol, obesity and a diet high in fat, meat, processed foods and sugar. It plays a major part in heart disease and strokes (see below) but many people don't even realise they have it.

A vegan diet can help prevent high blood pressure, with all its fibre, minerals and antioxidants – it is well-known that vegans have lower blood pressure than any other diet group (Alexander *et al.*, 2017; Chiu *et al.*, 2020). Compared with meat-eaters, vegans have a 63 per cent lower risk of high blood pressure (Pettersen *et al.*, 2012).

In people who suffer from high blood pressure, a switch to a wholefood plant-based diet usually achieves a significant blood pressure drop bringing it back to normal (Alexander *et al.*, 2017).

When it comes to other diets, science revealed that a vegan diet can achieve better results than a vegetarian one and is also better at keeping your blood pressure at a healthy level than low-fat diets that include animal products (Lee *et al.*, 2020; Jakše *et al.*, 2021)

KIDNEY DISEASE

Kidneys are working non-stop to remove waste products from the blood and flush them out in urine. What we eat determines how hard the kidneys have to work – and it just so happens that animal products tend to overload them while plants help to protect our kidney health.

Data from a study spanning over two decades suggest that animal protein from meat – red and processed in particular – is bad news for the kidneys, increasing the risk of kidney disease later in life by 23 per cent (Haring et al., 2017). The same study also revealed that plant protein from pulses and nuts has the opposite effect – it lowers the risk and seems to have a kidney-protective effect.

Other studies agree and it's been highlighted that it's not merely the origin of protein that matters – it's the total package of nutrients in plant foods that makes them so good for us and our kidneys (Gluba-Brzózka et al., 2017; Kalantar-Zadeh and Moore, 2019). A vegetarian or vegan diet can lower your risk of kidney disease by 13-16 per cent (Liu et al., 2019).

Plant foods produce less acid in the body than animal foods and they provide healthy alkaline salts that kidneys like. A wholesome vegan diet is so great for the kidneys that it's even recommended for people with kidney disease to prevent further damage (Gluba-Brzózka et al., 2017).

The same applies to kidney stones – diets based on plants slash your risk (Tourney et al., 2014). If you already suffer due to kidney stones, going vegan can prevent new ones from forming (Heilberg and Goldfarb, 2013).

LACTOSE INTOLERANCE

With lactose intolerance, the body can't digest the sugar in milk called lactose. It's found only in milk (all mammalian milk) and has to be broken down in the small intestine by an enzyme called lactase. No surprises, then, that it is only babies who normally have this enzyme and its production starts declining in early childhood when the toddler would be weaned. Nature didn't provide adults with it as they wouldn't need to drink milk after weaning.

The fact that some people can digest lactose in adulthood is down to several mutations in our history that removed this age-limit on lactase production.

In people who have lactose intolerance, undigested lactose reaches the large intestine where bacteria feast on it, creating gas and drawing water into the digestive tract. The result – bloating, stomach cramps, sometimes diarrhoea and always a lot of gas!

According to multiple studies, around 68 per cent of the world's population are lactose intolerant (Storhaug *et al.*, 2017). The lowest numbers are in Western Europe and USA – four to 36 per cent, while the highest are in Asia, Oceania, some Sub-Saharan African countries and some South American countries – 56 to 100 per cent!

This shows just how unnatural cow's milk really is for adults and why it plays a part in a host of diseases, including irritable bowel syndrome.

OBESITY

More and more people are obese which puts them at an increased risk of developing heart disease, high blood pressure, diabetes, arthritis, gallstones and some cancers. Being obese also weakens the immune system and so increases the recovery time after an illness or injury.

Scientific studies show that childhood obesity makes the the person likely to be obese also in adulthood (Simmonds et al., 2015; Desmond et al., 2018). Vegan and vegetarian children are usually within healthy weight ranges and less likely to be obese than meat-eating children (Desmond et al., 2018 and 2021).

When it comes to adults, wholefood vegan diets are extremely effective at achieving and maintaining a healthy weight, even without portion restriction (Huang et al., 2016; Turner-McGrievy et al., 2015 and 2017; Najjar and Feresin, 2019). Unlike all other diet groups, vegans have a consistently healthy body mass index (BMI) across studies and populations (Le and Sabaté, 2014; Najjar and Feresin, 2019).

OSTEOPOROSIS

Osteoporosis – porous or brittle bones – is the major cause of bone fractures in the elderly. The number of osteoporotic hip fractures in Western countries is alarming.

Despite our obsession with drinking cow's milk for calcium, supposedly to prevent osteoporosis, it isn't working. There's a distinct lack of studies that show beneficial effects of dairy consumption on bone health.

Bones need calcium but it certainly doesn't need to come from cow's milk! In fact, plant sources are better because your bones need a lot more nutrients and plants provide almost all of them. Just remember to take your vitamin D and B12 supplements.

Studies show that a diet rich in fruit and vegetables, calcium-fortified milk alternatives, nuts and grains is excellent for bone health (Movassagh et al., 2018). It's because these foods naturally contain nutrients essential for bones – protein, calcium, potassium, magnesium, vitamins A, C, K and folate.

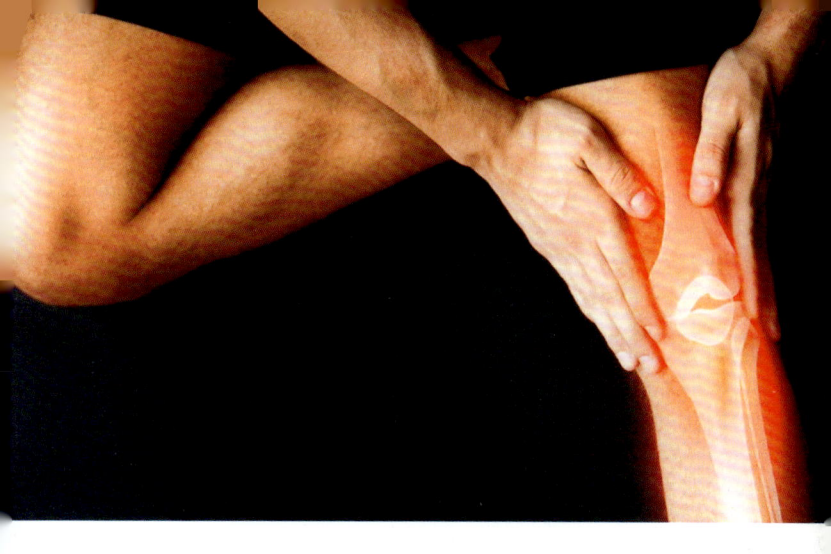

The high content of bone-beneficial nutrients in plant foods has been linked to good bone health of vegetarians and vegans (Knurick *et al.*, 2015; Sahni *et al.*, 2015; Burckhardt, 2016; Hsu, 2020). According to a major review by the US National Osteoporosis Foundation (Weaver *et al.*, 2016), bones need a good protein supply and plant protein does the job better than animal protein, which produces more acid in the body. The authors also concluded that fruit and vegetables have a positive effect on the bones, while carbonated (fizzy) drinks may have a negative effect. Lastly, they highlighted how important physical activity is for bone health, growth and development – bones need to be stimulated to grow and become stronger.

RHEUMATOID ARTHRITIS

Rheumatoid arthritis (RA) is a disease where the immune system attacks its own tissues – in this case cartilage and joint linings. The joints become inflamed, painful, stiff and may also swell.

A recent review neatly summarised the key diet elements increasing the risk of RA or making the symptoms worse – high intake of red meat, saturated and trans fats, refined carbohydrates (white flour, sugar), too much salt, alcohol and caffeine, too little omega-3 fats, and low intake of fibre, fruit and vegetables (Gioia *et al.*, 2020). On the other hand, the authors suggested that based on evidence, people should eat plenty of wholegrains, pulses, five or more servings of fruit and vegetables daily, omega-3 fats, extra virgin olive oil and take a vitamin D supplement to lower their risk of RA or to lessen its symptoms. This type of diet is not only healthy but also anti-inflammatory and can be extremely useful in combatting RA.

STROKE

A stroke is sudden damage to the brain caused by a blocked blood vessel resulting in a lack of blood supply or a blood vessel bursting, causing bleeding into the brain. Both scenarios mean that some part of the brain loses blood supply and is left without oxygen. Brain cells get damaged even after a few minutes without oxygen and when they die, the parts of the body they control cease to function.

In the UK, around 100,000 people suffer a stroke every year – that means one person every five minutes (Stroke Association, 2021).

There are many risk factors for stroke, including advanced age, high blood pressure, diabetes, high blood fats and cholesterol, smoking, physical inactivity, poor nutrition, obesity, coronary heart disease and depression (Campbell, 2017; Chiu *et al.*, 2020).

We can control many of these through diet and lifestyle – for example a healthy vegan diet is very effective at achieving healthy blood pressure (Alexander *et al.*, 2017; Lee *et al.*, 2020). Similarly, this type of diet can lower your cholesterol levels and reduce – even eliminate – cholesterol plaques in your blood vessels (Campbell, 2017). It is also anti-inflammatory and helps to support the healthy functioning of blood vessels.

According to several scientific studies, plant-based diets not only reduce the risk of heart disease and stroke, they also halt the progress of existing cardiovascular issues and may help you recover (Freeman *et al.*, 2017; Chiu *et al.*, 2020).

Children's Eating Habits

Why, when children are free to choose their own diet, do they choose the foods they do? The three main influences are habits, advertising or peer pressure, and their family's socioeconomic status – all need to be taken into account if kids are to have a healthy future.

By teaching your children how to eat well and look after their health, you're giving them a solid foundation to a healthy life.

Conclusions

As the hunger for Western diets consumes the world, it's becoming blindingly obvious what a health disaster it's caused and how many lives have needlessly been cut short because of it. Countless studies are documenting the epidemic of 'diseases of affluence' caused largely by eating too much meat, dairy, eggs and sugar. At the same time, vast numbers of studies are demonstrating just how powerful a diet change can be and how plant-based diets are supporting people's health all over the world.

By providing your child a well-planned vegan diet, you're giving them the best possible start to life. They won't only eat nourishing foods that are good for them, they'll also avoid a wealth of health-damaging compounds found only in animal-based foods and they'll be building healthy habits that can last a lifetime.

With the world's leading health and medical institutions advocating a move towards plant-based diets, there's no doubt that veganism is the future!

References

Abdull Razis AF, Noor NM. 2013. Cruciferous vegetables: dietary phytochemicals for cancer prevention. *Asian Pacific Journal of Cancer Prevention*. 14 (3) 1565-1570.

Agnoli C, Baroni L, Bertini I, *et al*. 2017. Position paper on vegetarian diets from the working group of the Italian Society of Human Nutrition. *Nutrition, Metabolism and Cardiovascular Diseases*. 27(12):1037-1052.

Alexander S, Ostfeld RJ, Allen K, Williams KA. 2017. A plant-based diet and hypertension. *Journal of Geriatric Cardiology*. 14(5): 327-330.

Alexy U, Fischer M, Weder S, *et al*. 2021. Nutrient Intake and Status of German Children and Adolescents Consuming Vegetarian, Vegan or Omnivore Diets: Results of the VeChi Youth Study. *Nutrients*. 13 (5): 1707.

Allen NE, Appleby PN, Davey GK, Kaaks R, Rinaldi S and Key TJ. 2002. The associations of diet with serum insulin-like growth factor I and its main binding proteins in 292 women meat-eaters, vegetarians, and vegans. *Cancer Epidemiology, Biomarkers & Prevention*. 11 (11): 1441- 1448.

Alvarez-Arellano L, Salazar-García M, Corona JC. 2020. Neuroprotective Effects of Quercetin in Pediatric Neurological Diseases. *Molecules*. 25 (23): 5597.

Ambroszkiewicz J, Chełchowska M, Rowicka G, *et al*. 2018. Anti-Inflammatory and Pro-Inflammatory Adipokine Profiles in Children on Vegetarian and Omnivorous Diets. *Nutrients*. 10(9):1241.

Amit M. 2010. Vegetarian diets in children and adolescents. *Paediatrics and Child Health*. 15(5):303-14.

Appleby PN, Key TJ. 2016. The Long-Term Health of Vegetarians and Vegans. *Proceedings of the Nutrition Society*. 75 (3) 287-293.

Applegate CC, Rowles JL, Ranard KM, *et al*. 2018. Soy Consumption and the Risk of Prostate Cancer: An Updated Systematic Review and Meta-Analysis. *Nutrients*. 10 (1): 40.

Arthritis Foundation. 2021. How to Eat an Anti-Inflammatory Diet for Juvenile Arthritis.

Aune D. 2019. Plant Foods, Antioxidant Biomarkers, and the Risk of Cardiovascular Disease, Cancer, and Mortality: A Review of the Evidence. *Advances in Nutrition*. 10 (Suppl_4): S404-S421.

Barnard ND, Cohen J, Jenkins DJ, Turner-McGrievy G, Gloede L, Green A and Ferdowsian H. 2009. A low-fat vegan diet and conventional diabetes diet in the treatment of type 2 diabetes: a randomized, controlled, 74-wk clinical trial. *American Journal of Clinical Nutrition*. 89 (5) 1588S-1596S.

Baroni L, Goggi S, Battaglino R, *et al*. 2018. Vegan Nutrition for Mothers and Children: Practical Tools for Healthcare Providers. *Nutrients*. 11(1):5.

Benatar JR and Stewart RAH. 2018. Cardiometabolic risk factors in vegans; A meta-analysis of observational studies. *PLoS One*. 13 (12) e0209086.

Blacklock CJ, Lawrence JR, Wiles D, *et al* 2001. Salicylic acid in the serum of subjects not taking aspirin. Comparison of salicylic acid concentrations in the serum of vegetarians, non-vegetarians, and patients taking low dose aspirin. *Journal of Clinical Pathology*. 54 (7): 553-5.

Bong J, Kang HW, Cho H, *et al*. 2020. Vegetarianism as a protective factor for asymptomatic colonic diverticulosis in Asians: a retrospective cross-sectional and case-control study. *Intestinal Research*. 18 (1): 121-129.

Bosch AC, O'Neill B, Sigge GO, Kerwath SE, Hoffman LC. 2016. Heavy metals in marine fish meat and consumer health: a review. *Journal of the Science of Food and Agriculture*. 96 (1) 32-48.

Bosetti C, Filomeno M, Riso P, *et al*. 2012. Cruciferous vegetables and cancer risk in a network of case-control studies. *Annals of Oncology*. 23 (8) 2198-2203.

Bouvard V, Loomis D, Guyton KZ, *et al*., International Agency for Research on Cancer Monograph Working Group. 2015. Carcinogenicity of consumption of red and processed meat. *The Lancet Oncology*. 16(16): 1599-600.

Bradbury KE, Crowe FL, Appleby PN *et al*. 2014. Serum concentrations of cholesterol, apolipoprotein A-I and apolipoprotein B in a total of 1694 meat-eaters, fish-eaters, vegetarians and vegans. *European Journal of Clinical Nutrition*. 68 (2) 178-183.

British Heart Foundation (BHF). 2021. UK Factsheet – July 2021.

Buja A, Pierbon M, Lago L, Grotto G, Baldo V. 2020. Breast Cancer Primary Prevention and Diet: An Umbrella Review. *Internationl Journal of Environonmental Research and Public Health*. 17 (13): 4731.

Campbell T. 2017. A plant-based diet and stroke. *Journal of Geriatric Cardiology*. 14(5):321-326.

Cancer Research UK (CRUK). 2020. Cancer incidence statistics. Available at: www.cancerresearchuk.org/health-professional/cancer-statistics/

Chang CM, Chiu THT, Chang CC, Lin MN, Lin CL. 2019. Plant-Based Diet, Cholesterol, and Risk of Gallstone Disease: A Prospective Study. *Nutrients*. 11 (2): 335.

Chia JSJ, McRae JL, Kukuljan S, *et al*. 2017. A1 beta-casein milk protein and other environmental pre-disposing factors for type 1 diabetes. *Nutrition and Diabetes*. 7(5):e274.

Chiu THT, Chang HR, Wang LY, *et al*. 2020. Vegetarian diet and incidence of total, ischemic, and hemorrhagic stroke in 2 cohorts in Taiwan. *Neurology*. 94(11):e1112-e1121.

Crowe FL, Appleby PN, Allen NE and Key TJ. 2011. Diet and risk of diverticular disease in Oxford cohort of European Prospective Investigation into Cancer and Nutrition (EPIC): prospective study of British vegetarians and non-vegetarians. *BMJ*. 343: d4131.

DEFRA. 2020. The Expert Committee on Pesticide Residues in Food (PRiF) Annual Report 2020.

Desmond MA, Sobiecki J, Fewtrell M, Wells JCK. 2018. Plant-based diets for children as a means of improving adult cardiometabolic health. *Nutrition Reviews*. 76(4):260-273.

Desmond MA, Sobiecki JG, Jaworski M, *et al*. 2021. Growth, body composition, and cardiovascular and nutritional risk of 5- to 10-y-old children consuming vegetarian, vegan, or omnivore diets. *American Journal of Clinical Nutrition*. 113 (6): 1565-1577.

Diabetes, UK. 2019. Tackling the crisis: Transforming diabetes care for a better future England.

Dinu M, Abbate R, Gensini GF, Casini A, Sofi F. 2017. Vegetarian, vegan diets and multiple health outcomes: A systematic review with meta-analysis of observational studies. *Critical Reviews in Food Science and Nutrition*. 57(17): 3640-3649.

Esselstyn CB Jr, Gendy G, Doyle J *et al*. 2014. A way to reverse CAD?. *Journal of Family Practice*. 63 (7) 356-364b.

Gaby AR. 2009. Nutritional approaches to prevention and treatment of gallstones. *Alternative Medicine Reviews*.14 (3): 258-67.

Gluba-Brzózka A, Franczyk B, Rysz J. 2017. Vegetarian Diet in Chronic Kidney Disease-A Friend or Foe. *Nutrients*. 9 (4) 374.

Heilberg IP and Goldfarb DS. 2013. Optimum nutrition for kidney stone disease. *Advanced Chronic Kidney Disease*. 20 (2) 165-174.

Huang T, Yang B, Zheng J, Li G, Wahlqvist ML and Li D. 2012. Cardiovascular disease mortality and cancer incidence in vegetarians: a meta-analysis and systematic review. *Annals of Nutrition and Metabolism*. 60 (4) 233-240.

Fraser GE, Jaceldo-Siegl K, Orlich M, *et al*. 2020. Dairy, soy, and risk of breast cancer: those confounded milks. *International Journal of Epidemiology*. 49 (5): 1526-1537.

Freeman AM, Morris PB, Aspry K, *et al*. 2018. A Clinician's Guide for Trending Cardiovascular Nutrition Controversies: Part II. *Journal of the American College of Cardiology*. 72(5): 553-568.

FSA. 2020. Foodborne Disease Estimates for the United Kingdom in 2018.

Ganmaa D and Sato A, 2005. The possible role of female sex hormones in milk from pregnant cows in the development of breast, ovarian and corpus uteri cancers. *Medical Hypotheses*. 65:1028–37.

GBD 2017 Diet Collaborators. 2019. Health effects of dietary risks in 195 countries, 1990-2017: a systematic analysis for the Global Burden of Disease Study 2017. *Lancet*. 393 (10184): 1958-1972.

GBD 2017 Risk Factor Collaborators. 2018. Global, regional, and national comparative risk assessment of 84 behavioural, environmental and occupational, and metabolic risks or clusters of risks for 195 countries and territories, 1990-2017: a systematic analysis for the Global Burden of Disease Study 2017. *Lancet*. 392 (10159): 1923-1994.

Gioia C, Lucchino B, Tarsitano MG, *et al*. 2020. Dietary Habits and Nutrition in Rheumatoid Arthritis: Can Diet Influence Disease Development and Clinical Manifestations? *Nutrients*. 12 (5): 1456.

Grosvenor CE, Picciano MF and Baumrucker CR. 1992. Hormones and growth factors in milk. *Endocrine Reviews*. 14 (6) 710-728.

Guasch-Ferré M, Hu FB, Martínez-González MA, *et al*. 2014. Olive oil intake and risk of cardiovascular disease and mortality in the PREDIMED Study. *BMC Medicine*. 12:78.

Guéguen M, Amiard JC, Arnich N, Badot PM, Claisse D, Guérin T, Vernoux JP. 2011. Shellfish and residual chemical contaminants: hazards, monitoring, and health risk assessment along French coasts. *Reviews of Environmental Contamination and Toxicology*. 213: 55-111.

Halvorsrud K, Lewney J, Craig D, Moynihan PJ. 2019. Effects of Starch on Oral Health: Systematic Review to Inform WHO Guideline. *Journal of Dental Research*. 98 (1): 46-53.

Haring B, Selvin E, Liang M, *et al*. 2017. Dietary Protein Sources and Risk for Incident Chronic Kidney Disease: Results From the Atherosclerosis Risk in Communities (ARIC) Study. *Journal of Renal Nutrition*. 27 (4) 233–242.

Hsu E. 2020. Plant-based diets and bone health: sorting through the evidence. *Current Opinions in Endocrinology, Diabetes and Obesity*. 27 (4): 248-252.

Huang RY, Huang CC, Hu FB *et al*. 2016. Vegetarian Diets and Weight Reduction: a Meta-Analysis of Randomized Controlled Trials. *Journal of General Internal Medicine*. 31 (1) 109-116.

Jakše B, Jakše B, Godnov U, Pinter S. 2021. Nutritional, Cardiovascular Health and Lifestyle Status of 'Health Conscious' Adult Vegans and Non-Vegans from Slovenia: A Cross-Sectional Self-Reported Survey. *International Journal of Environmental Research and Public Health*. 18 (11): 5968.

Jansen PR, Petrus NCM, Venema A, *et al*. 2018. Higher Polygenetic Predisposition for Asthma in Cow's Milk Allergic Children. *Nutrients*. 10 (11): 1582.

Jenkins DJA, Blanco Mejia S, Chiavaroli L, *et al*. 2019. Cumulative Meta-Analysis of the Soy Effect Over Time. *Journal of the American Heart Association*. 8 (13): e012458.

Kahleova H, Matoulek M, Malinska H *et al*. 2011. Vegetarian diet improves insulin resistance and oxidative stress markers more than conventional diet in subjects with Type 2 diabetes. *Diabetes Medicine*. 28 (5) 549 559.

Kahleova H, Tura A, Hill M *et al*. 2018. A Plant-Based Dietary Intervention Improves Beta-Cell Function and Insulin Resistance in Overweight Adults: A 16-Week Randomized Clinical Trial. *Nutrients*. 10 (2) 189.

Kalantar-Zadeh K, Moore LW. 2019. Does Kidney Longevity Mean Healthy Vegan Food and Less Meat or Is Any Low-Protein Diet Good Enough?. *Journal of Renal Nutrition*. 29 (2) 79–81.

Knurick JR, Johnston CS, Wherry SJ, Aguayo I. 2015. Comparison of correlates of bone mineral density in individuals adhering to lacto-ovo, vegan, or omnivore diets: a cross-sectional investigation. *Nutrients*. 7 (5): 3416-3426.

Korakas E, Dimitriadis G, Raptis A, Lambadiari V. 2018. Dietary Composition and Cardiovascular Risk: A Mediator or a Bystander? *Nutrients*. 10 (12): 1912.

Key TJ, Appleby PN, Crowe FL, Bradbury KE, Schmidt JA, Travis RC. 2014. Cancer in British vegetarians: updated analyses of 4998 incident cancers in a cohort of 32,491 meat eaters, 8612 fish eaters, 18,298 vegetarians, and 2246 vegans. *American Journal of Clinical Nutrition*. 100 Suppl 1:378S-385S.

Key TJ, Bradbury KE, Perez-Cornago A, *et al*. 2020. Diet, nutrition, and cancer risk: what do we know and what is the way forward? *British Medical Journal*. 368:m511.

Le LT, Sabaté J. 2014. Beyond meatless, the health effects of vegan diets: findings from the Adventist cohorts. *Nutrients*. 6(6):2131-2147.

Lee KW, Loh HC, Ching SM, Devaraj NK, Hoo FK. 2020. Effects of Vegetarian Diets on Blood Pressure Lowering: A Systematic Review with Meta-Analysis and Trial Sequential Analysis. *Nutrients*. 12(6):1604.

Lemale J, Mas E, Jung C, Bellaiche M, Tounian P. French-speaking Pediatric Hepatology, Gastroenterology and Nutrition Group (GFHGNP). 2019. Vegan diet in children and adolescents. Recommendations from the French-speaking Pediatric Hepatology, Gastroenterology and Nutrition Group (GFHGNP). *Archives de Pediatrie*. 26 (7): 442-450.

Liu HW, Tsai WH, Liu JS, Kuo KL. 2019. Association of Vegetarian Diet with Chronic Kidney Disease. *Nutrients*. 11 (2): 279.

Lund BM. 2015. Microbiological Food Safety for Vulnerable People. *International Journal of Environmental Research and Public Health*. 12 (8): 10117-10132.

Mandair D, Rossi RE, Pericleous M, Whyand T, Caplin ME. 2014. Prostate cancer and the influence of dietary factors and supplements: a systematic review. *Nutrition and Metabolism (Lond)*. 11: 30.

Marcotrigiano GO, Storelli MM. 2003. Heavy metal, polychlorinated biphenyl and organochlorine pesticide residues in marine organisms: risk evaluation for consumers. *Veterinary Research Communication*. 27 Suppl 1:183-95.

Martínez-González MA, Sánchez-Tainta A, Corella D, *et al*. PREDIMED Group. 2014. A provegetarian food pattern and reduction in total mortality in the Prevención con Dieta Mediterránea (PREDIMED) study. *American Journal of Clinical Nutrition*. 100 Suppl 1:320S-328S.

Matsumoto S, Beeson WL, Shavlik DJ, Siapco G, Jaceldo-Siegl K, Fraser G, Knutsen SF. 2019. Association between vegetarian diets and cardiovascular risk factors in non-Hispanic white participants of the Adventist Health Study-2. *Journal of Nutrition Science*. 8:e6.

McCarty MF. 2014. GCN2 and FGF21 are likely mediators of the protection from cancer, autoimmunity, obesity, and diabetes afforded by vegan diets. *Medical Hypotheses*. 83 (3) 365–371.

McCarty MF. 2017. Plant-based diets relatively low in bioavailable phosphate and calcium may aid prevention and control of prostate cancer by lessening production of fibroblast growth factor 23. *Medical Hypotheses*. 99: 68-72.

McMacken M, Shah S. 2017. A plant-based diet for the prevention and treatment of type 2 diabetes. *Journal of Geriatric Cardiology*. 14 (5): 342–354

Melina V, Craig W, Levin S. 2016. Position of the Academy of Nutrition and Dietetics: Vegetarian Diets. *Journal of the Academy of Nutrition and Dietetics*. 116(12):1970-1980

Messina M. 2016. Soy and Health Update: Evaluation of the Clinical and Epidemiologic Literature. *Nutrients*. 8 (12): 754.

Mosby TT, Cosgrove M, Sarkardei S, Platt KL, Kaina B. 2012. Nutrition in adult and childhood cancer: role of carcinogens and anti-carcinogens. *Anticancer Research*. 32 (10): 4171-4192.

Movassagh EZ, Baxter-Jones ADG, Kontulainen S, Whiting S, Szafron M, Vatanparast H. 2018. Vegetarian-style dietary pattern during adolescence has long-term positive impact on bone from adolescence to young adulthood: a longitudinal study. *Nutrition Journal*. 17 (1): 36.

Murphy N, Norat T, Ferrari P, Jenab M *et al*. 2012. Dietary fibre intake and risks of cancers of the colon and rectum in the European prospective investigation into cancer and nutrition (EPIC). *PLoS One*. 7 (6): e39361.

Najjar RS, Feresin RG. 2019. Plant-Based Diets in the Reduction of Body Fat: Physiological Effects and Biochemical Insights. *Nutrients*. 11(11):2712.

Naser SA, Sagramsingh SR, Naser AS, Thanigachalam S. 2014. Mycobacterium avium subspecies paratuberculosis causes Crohn's disease in some inflammatory bowel disease patients. *World Journal of Gastroenterology*. 20 (23): 7403-7415.

NHS. 2020. National Child Measurement Programme, England 2019/20 School Year.

O'Keefe SJ. 2016. Diet, microorganisms and their metabolites, and colon cancer. Nature Reviews. *Gastroenterology and Hepatology*. 13 (12): 691-706.

Orlich MJ, Singh PN, Sabaté J, *et al*. 2013. Vegetarian dietary patterns and mortality in Adventist Health Study 2. *JAMA Internal Medicine*. 173 (13): 1230-1238.

Pettersen BJ, Anousheh R, Fan J, Jaceldo-Siegl K, Fraser GE. 2012. Vegetarian diets and blood pressure among white subjects: results from the Adventist Health Study-2 (AHS-2). *Public Health Nutrition*. 15(10):1909-1916.

PHE. 2019. APRHAI 9th annual report.

PHE. 2020. National Diet and Nutrition Survey Rolling programme Years 9 to 11 (2016/2017 to 2018/2019).

Rizzo G and Baroni L. 2018. Soy, Soy Foods and Their Role in Vegetarian Diets. *Nutrients*. 10 (1): 43.

Romo Ventura E, Konigorski S, Rohrmann S, *et al*. 2020. Association of dietary intake of milk and dairy products with blood concentrations of insulin-like growth factor 1 (IGF-1) in Bavarian adults. *European Journal of Nutrition*. 59 (4): 1413-1420.

Sahni S, Mangano KM, McLean RR, Hannan MT, Kiel DP. 2015. Dietary Approaches for Bone Health: Lessons from the Framingham Osteoporosis Study. *Current Osteoporosis Reports*. 13 (4) 245–255.

Salas-Salvadó J, Becerra-Tomás N, Papandreou C, Bulló M. 2019. Dietary Patterns Emphasizing the Consumption of Plant Foods in the Management of Type 2 Diabetes: A Narrative Review. *Advances in Nutrition*. 10 (Suppl_4): S320 \S331.

Saunders AV, Craig WJ, Baines SK, Posen JS. 2013. Iron and vegetarian diets. *The Medical Journal of Australia*. 199 (S4): S11-6.

Savadatti SS, Liu M, Caglayan C, Reuther J, Lewis-Michl EL, *et al*. 2019. Biomonitoring of populations in Western New York at risk for exposure to Great Lakes contaminants. *Environmental Research*. 179(Pt A):108690.

Segovia-Siapco G and Sabaté J. 2019. Health and sustainability outcomes of vegetarian dietary patterns: a revisit of the EPIC-Oxford and the Adventist Health Study-2 cohorts. *European Journal of Clinical Nutrition*. 72(Suppl 1):60-70.

Serbis A, Giapros V, Kotanidou EP, Galli-Tsinopoulou A, Siomou E. 2021. Diagnosis, treatment and prevention of type 2 diabetes mellitus in children and adolescents. *World Journal of Diabetes*. 12 (4): 344-365.

Sharma A, Kaur M, Katnoria JK, Nagpal AK. 2018. Polyphenols in Food: Cancer Prevention and Apoptosis Induction. *Current Medicinal Chemistry*. 25 (36): 4740-4757.

Shin S, Saito E, Inoue M, *et al*. 2016. Dietary pattern and breast cancer risk in Japanese women: the Japan Public Health Center-based Prospective Study (JPHC Study). *British Journal of Nutrition*. 115 (10): 1769-79.

Simmonds M, Burch J, Llewellyn A, *et al*. 2015. The use of measures of obesity in childhood for predicting obesity and the development of obesity-related diseases in adulthood: a systematic review and meta-analysis. *Health Technology Assessment*. 19 (43): 1-336.

Storhaug CL, Fosse SK, Fadnes LT. 2017. Country, regional, and global estimates for lactose malabsorption in adults: a systematic review and meta-analysis. *Lancet Gastroenterology and Hepatology*. 2: 738–46.

Stroke Association. 2021. Stroke Statistics. Available at: www.stroke.org.uk/what-is-stroke/stroke-statistics

Tantamango-Bartley Y, Jaceldo-Siegl K, Fan J, Fraser G. 2013. Vegetarian diets and the incidence of cancer in a low-risk population. 2013. *Cancer Epidemiology, Biomarkers & Prevention*. 22 (2): 286-294.

Tantamango-Bartley Y, Knutsen SF, Knutsen R, *et al*. 2016. Are strict vegetarians protected against prostate cancer? *American Journal of Clinical Nutrition*. 103 (1): 153-60.

Turner-McGrievy GM, Davidson CR, Wingard EE, Wilcox S, Frongillo EA. 2015. Comparative effectiveness of plant-based diets for weight loss: a randomized controlled trial of five different diets. *Nutrition*. 31(2):350-358.

Turner-McGrievy G, Mandes T, Crimarco A. 2017. A plant-based diet for overweight and obesity prevention and treatment. *Journal of Geriatric Cardiology*. 14(5):369-374.

Turney BW, Appleby PN, Reynard JM, Noble JG, Key TJ and Allen NE. 2014. Diet and risk of kidney stones in the Oxford cohort of the European Prospective Investigation into Cancer and Nutrition (EPIC). *European Journal of Epidemiology*. 29 (5) 363-369.

Weaver CM, Gordon CM, Janz KF, *et al*. 2016. The National Osteoporosis Foundation's position statement on peak bone mass development and lifestyle factors: a systematic review and implementation recommendations. *Osteoporosis International*. 27 (4): 1281-1386.

Wolk A. 2017. Potential health hazards of eating red meat (Review). *Journal of Internal Medicine*. 281: 106–122.

World Cancer Research Fund (WCRF). 2018. *Diet, Nutrition, Physical Activity and Cancer: A Global Perspective*. Continuous Update Project Expert Report 2018.

Zennegg M. 2018. Dioxins and PCBs in Meat – Still a Matter of Concern? *Chimia (Aarau)*. 72 (10): 690-696.